D1474924

Flying for Peanuts

Hope you enjoy!
Fly well!!
Best,
Marty Thompson

FIVE STAR PUBLICATIONS, INC

Chandler, Arizona

Flying for Peanuts

by
MARTY THOMPSON

illustrations by JEFF YESH

Five Star Publications, Inc.
PO Box 6698   Chandler, AZ 85246-6698
tel (480) 940-8182   **fax** (480) 940-8787
www.FiveStarPublications.com
peanuts@FiveStarPublications.com
www.FiveStarPublications.com/books/flyingforpeanuts

Library of Congress Cataloging-in-Publication Data

Thompson, Marty, 1949-
 Flying for peanuts : the A, B, C's of flying Southwest Airlines /
Marty Thompson.
     p. cm.
  ISBN 1-58985-006-8
  1. Southwest Airlines Co.--Humor. 2. Airlines--United States--Humor.
I. Title.
  HE9803.S68T48 2004
  387.7'0973--dc22

                                                         2003019758

Permissions

Pages 9, 18, and 109: From *Bound By Love, Rather Than Fear* by Michael Wilson in *Benefits & Compensation Solutions, an in-depth business magazine for benefits and compensation managers*—www.bcsolutionsmag.com. Reprinted by permission.

Material cited to Southwest Airlines is reproduced courtesy of Southwest Airlines.

Page 137: From *Some flight attendants get silly for safety's sake* in *The Arizona Republic*. Reprinted with permission of The Associated Press.

Page 146: From *Laughter often a sign of best companies* by Dale Dauten in *The Arizona Republic*, November 20, 2001. Reprinted by permission of King Features Syndicate.

Kings Delicious Nuts® is a registered trademark of the King Nut Companies.

Wild Turkey® is a registered trademark of Austin Nichols and Company.

PUBLISHER
Linda F. Radke

EDITOR
Gary Anderson

PROJECT MANAGER
Sue DeFabis

COVER DESIGN AND
COMPOSITION
Barbara Kordesh

ILLUSTRATIONS
Jeff Yesh

Dedication

This flight manual is dedicated to Herbert D. Kelleher, Chairman of the Board of Directors and founder of Southwest Airlines. Herb has coached his management team and "People" into a winner. Not just a financial winner for the Company, but also a champion for the average American flyer.

He has done so by inspiring a blue-collar work ethic and a friendly sense of humor throughout the organization. As a result, all who fly Southwest have become winners, as well.

Herb is one of few people who could appreciate a work of this caliber.

"FLYING FOR PEANUTS IS THE ONLY FLIGHT MANUAL EVER PUBLISHED THAT TEACHES THE SKILLS NECESSARY TO MANAGE YOUR OWN CUSTOMER SERVICE."

—MARTY THOMPSON
ARIZONA MENTAL INSTITUTION
JANUARY 2003

Acknowledgement

The following individuals share in the blame for making this book a reality.

At Five Star Publications, Inc., Linda Radke and Sue DeFabis are at fault for their constant nagging about details and form. Due to their professional touches and creative input my true abilities were completely disguised.

Illustrator, Jeff Yesh, is to blame for the outlandish sketches he prepared for this book. His exceptional skill and artistic talent brought life to the book, thus diverting the reader from noticing the quality of writing.

Barbara Kordesh shares in the blame, as she designed the manuscript to look appealing, professional and appear to be a real book. Having applied her expertise, the book now looks nothing like the copy I compelled her to work with.

True culpability lies with my parents, Mike and Anne, who are the greatest parents in the world, but initiated the early development of my weird psychological difficulties by forcing me to get a job.

I blame my wife Jackie for not acting on her inclination to have me committed for my bizarre disposition. Her patience and tolerance of my way of thinking only encouraged me to continue my eccentric perspective.

I apologize to my sons, Marty and Jason, for any public humiliation they may suffer as a result of this publication.

About the Author

Marty Thompson is just your average American blue-collar working stiff. Although he has held such white-collar positions as Director, V. P. of Human Resources, V.P. of Manufacturing and Chief Operating Officer in the steel, banking and foods industries, his father was disappointed that he didn't become a welder.

Thompson has some degrees from the University of Wisconsin, but he's most proud of having finished high school.

Thompson's unorthodox observation techniques lend themselves perfectly to his curious writing style. His business perspective entails the purging of surveys, consultants, and humorless customers from the customer service process.

His field research for "Flying for Peanuts" came from decades of pointless business travel—most often on Southwest Airlines. Fascinated by the airline's success and their lack of a textbook customer service protocol, Thompson has meticulously documented Southwest's methods in this hilarious book.

"Flying for Peanuts" is truly a flight of fancy, and readers will find Marty Thompson's business acumen and extensive education neatly disguised by his classless sense of humor.

Foreword

Southwest Airlines is America's Airline!

Since the early 70's Southwest has provided the average American an economical way to fly. Most of us work hard just to make a living and the thought of buying airline tickets for the family leaves us a bit ouchy. For over thirty years this airline has given the typical hardworking guy or gal an affordable means of flying.

Southwest does not operate like other airlines. No assigned seating, no meals, no first class and no hard-to-figure fares. What they do provide are evenhanded ticket prices, on time arrivals, and a humorous, fun approach to the serious matter of flying.

In my opinion, just give us customers a good deal and we will find our own seats and bring our own meals! Whether it's a family on a tight budget or a business trying to hold down overhead, all we want is a reasonable chance to fly without going bankrupt.

By creating an efficient, low-cost, people-oriented organization, Southwest has maintained a reasonable ticket price, giving us regular Americans a chance to fly. Their employees are helpful, down-to-earth, and provide a concerned connection between passengers and the airline.

Passengers value the way they are treated. It has been my experience that the majority of airlines do not display the same working class attitude as does Southwest.

That's why it's time to give Southwest its due as "America's Airline."

This flight manual is written employing the same style of humor used by Southwest in its manner of doing business. Nuts! Southwest operates under the theme, "LUV." The premise of this manual is "Crazy LUV." It is intended to provide some humorous "power to the people" easy reading on a typical short flight.

With all due respect, please note that this is the last serious accolade I can compel myself to make in this flight manual. I think it's my medication.

SOUTHWEST STOCK IS LISTED ON THE NEW YORK STOCK EXCHANGE AS "LUV."

In Honor of Irma

Irma has never been properly credited for her contributions to the airline industry. In 1909, before the U.S. Postmaster ever thought of "Air Mail," she flew a North Dakota mail route between Fargo and Lakota—at the age of 15. In 1922, she and her husband Sven established AirFin Airlines, the first commercial airline, out of Fergus Falls, MN. Sven was the pilot of a custom-made six-passenger Junker F-13 airplane, and Irma advertised and sold tickets. On that maiden flight in February 1922, Irma became the first airline stewardess to work a commercial flight. She invented customer service long before other airlines even considered the concept.

Outliving AirFin and Sven, Irma worked as a flight attendant for over eighty years, retiring in 2002 from Yucatan Airlines. During that time she wrote the book on customer service! As a customer service guru, she trained over 367,000 flight attendants, wrote 67 books on customer service and offered consulting services to every major airline in the world. The woman knew how to take care of a passenger!

The author was fortunate enough to meet Irma on a Southwest flight in June of 2002. The ensuing conversation resulted in a publication that will revolutionize customer service in the airline industry. Her concept was simple; the passengers, not the airline, truly dictate customer service.

Passengers need only take the service they want. Irma's genius influenced this flight manual.

Her observation was that Southwest Airlines is the only airline in the industry that has the unique organizational structure that allows passengers the freedom to determine their own level of service. Great flight scheduling, well-trained employees, weird management and a loving attitude. (Irma insisted that her feelings about Southwest had nothing to do with that cute young Herb fella.) Irma suggested to the author a few simple step-by-step techniques passengers can easily understand and utilize to create the level of service they desire.

Without Irma's keen insights into customer service, this remarkable piece of work could never have been written. In this manual, Irma personally demonstrates to the best of her ability, several techniques passengers may employ to gain the type of customer service heretofore only granted to royalty.

Over her decades of service to the airline industry, Irma has received thousands of awards for her tireless effort to improve customer service. It was an honor to work with such a dedicated, kind, gentle and loving icon as Irma. Sadly, Irma passed away in March 2003, while reviewing the final draft of the "Flying for Peanuts" manuscript. I will always feel somewhat responsible for her untimely passing. Of course, it may have been her karma for all the people she used to beat with that darn cane of hers. In any event, I'm sure Irma has found true happiness in that big bird high in the sky.

Note Admittedly, Irma was not impressed with my work as an author. Her blunt assessment pointed out such failings as, "sloppy, poor detail, bad grammar, bad facts, careless, shoddy, lackadaisical and relatively inferior." Having been humbled by her expressions, I agreed that she could articulate her candid opinion in memo form at the end of each chapter (*The Spirit of Irma*)—hoping to appease her a bit. What a mistake! I should have just taken the cane beating she likely would have administered and got it over with.

Irma—A True All-American

Irma's been an All-American so she knew one when she saw one. She never hid her great love for her country and her work—or for that matter anything else! She considered herself a plain talking, hard working, hard drinking, no nonsense American woman. She was the sweetest woman you could ever know, but if anyone made her mad...Irma had that American "Spirit."

Irma's wooden cane was her trademark. In her mind it was more than just a disciplinary tool. It was a sturdy utensil that could be used to persuade the uncooperative public.

In 1941 Irma volunteered to instruct Army
paratroopers on the dangerous skill of night
jumping. A skill she perfected. One cold, snowy
night her chute failed to open, resulting in a
nasty broken leg. Lieutenant Colonel Dwight D.
Eisenhower visited her in the hospital the next
day. He presented her with his cane to use until
she recovered. Her limp and cane came to
symbolize the American will to triumph.

Spirit of Irma

Listen up,

Americans like a straight shooter. These people give ya what they advertise, no B. S.! I was the first person bright enough to figure out that Southwest is the "right" airline for the typical red, white and blue American. And, dang it, I'm here to tell ya, shape up and fly "right."

Lots' a Luck,

Irma

"THEY HUG, KISS, CRY, AND SAY, 'LOVE YOU' ON THE JOB. FOR THIS..."

—*NUTS!: SOUTHWEST AIRLINES' CRAZY RECIPE
FOR BUSINESS AND PERSONAL SUCCESS*
FREIBERG

Preface

Southwest runs a very unique business! No airline customer service concept is as solidly founded on the premise that flying can be fun for both the passenger and the airline employees, except Southwest. As a matter of fact, in today's business climate, Southwest is probably the only carrier in the airline industry that is, indeed, having any fun at all!

This manual enlightens the traveling public on the relationship that has evolved between Southwest Airlines and its customers. Their claim to fame, being a "fun" or "love" airline, implies "family" to the customer. In reality, they have less of a customer service attitude and more of a brother—sister manner of showing affection. Not only is that unique, but as you know, siblings enjoy a good laugh at the other's expense. To truly understand the Southwest relationship with its customers, look at your own family. Ever poke fun at your weird brother?

There aren't many airlines that let the passengers have a shot at a little fun. Southwest provides a few passenger opportunities for fun, but they still like to maintain control. Many of us passengers are just as strange as Southwest employees. As a matter of fact, many employees say passengers are downright crazy! That's the type of compliment I enjoy.

It would seem to the keen observer, though, that Southwest employees are having more fun than their passengers. Whose fault is that? Not Southwest employees; they are trained to have fun —and to create an environment for fun things to happen, mostly with passengers. Maybe it is time for passengers to take a lesson from these people. Maybe it is time to turn the tables. Maybe it is time passengers told a few corny jokes, pulled a few crazy stunts!

Although targeted at passengers, this manual can benefit Southwest employees, as well. They too must be enlightened to the fact that passengers are learning to have fun, utilizing unique entertainment strategies of their own. Thus, this work has become a vehicle for a wide audience of travelers. In other words, everyone is going to know what is really going on under the promotional banner of being a "fun" and "love" airline.

Now, it's true that I am a reasonably loyal customer of Southwest; nevertheless I'm still obligated to the reading public to write it the way I see it. This manual is based on questionable sources and opinionated facts. My research might have been limited to materials found in the seat backs, but once I did skim a book on the Wright Brothers. Herb probably questions my expertise as regards his company; but so what, I don't know anything about the other airlines, either. Truth is, this manual is by a passenger, for a passenger. Southwest just happens to be a good place to teach what this work offers the learner.

Hopefully, this totally true, fictional manual will encourage you to learn about, and to experiment with the "power of the passenger". As a result, your flight experience will be on your terms. What are they gonna do—throw momma off the plane?

Contents

Introduction

I'VE FLOWN EVERY MAJOR AIRLINE CARRIER in the country
over the past twenty-five years and have been on
several frequent flyer programs. Astonishingly, I
have witnessed on-time flights, uninjured baggage
and accurate flight information. On several occasions, I have been the victim of an outstanding
act of customer service.

Basically, I know the *joys* of flying and have
pretty well seen it all. For years, I was like every
other passenger. I walked through ticketing,
baggage, check-in, boarding and seating like a pre-
programmed robot. Doing as directed and only

changing my demeanor when I could take no more abuse; then there was a very ugly display of futility as some airline employee was the recipient of my wrath. It has been particularly infuriating when I've caught them glancing at their watch, more concerned about quitting time than my stupid problems.

While I may have seen it all, I never really *looked* at what was going on around me. A few years ago, it happened in El Paso while I was sitting in the airport lounge, just watching. Yes, another delay. As I sipped my fifteen-dollar cocktail, it hit me. A rum induced vision. There is a method to the airline industry's madness! Secrets I bet few airline employees realize and passengers have yet to discover. Knowledge revealed to me for the simple price of a dozen drinks.

With my newfound knowledge, I elevate *myself* to a new level of customer satisfaction. I see clearly what is going on. I still may be forced into the "push and shove," "hurry and wait," "sure we are on time" shades of truth announcements by the airline world, but I now view events through the eyes of a much wiser passenger. I know what they are up to! I understand what those who attempt to manage our flight experience are doing to us.

Rarely is it airline employees that make air travel a happy or miserable event. It is primarily the passengers themselves—feeding on their own kind—that determine the flying experience. According to PropPassenger magazine, statistics show that "ninety-two percent of flight travel misery stems from passenger actions, not airline employee abuse." Therein lies the ugly truth uninformed travelers must accept. The reality is that we as passengers truly can create the flight experience we want. With that knowledge, the answer is simple; develop control, manipulation and intimidation skills. Only then can we secure the loving flight experience we deserve!

The airline industry manages the flight experience by attempting to create situations for lively, fired up passengers to provide employee entertainment, thus preventing on-the-job boredom. Call it an employee benefit. All airlines do it. Some try to be classy, some snooty and arrogant, others even try to hide it by acting irritated. Basically, though, all have failed to get the most enjoyment from passenger stupidity—except one.

Southwest Airlines probably has the best value in the business when it comes to ticket prices. To offer low-cost, "fly-for-peanuts" fares, Southwest has done away with most of the gimmicks used by their competitors. They have also created a unique system that makes the passenger accountable for their flight experience.

 **Note** By nature, people hate accountability, but love peanuts!

If you make a reservation early, you get a better deal than the day before the flight. But, after that, it is a level playing field; every passenger has the same shot at determining their own comfort. One passenger is no more special than another. Really, this is where Southwest is unique.

The way they hire also distinguishes the airline. Southwest employees are very special people. People are carefully selected to fit into the Southwest culture of customer service. They have been very successful in hiring people who think life is about love and fun. Have you ever met anyone that thinks that way? Let's look at the numbers. In 2002, Southwest received 243,657 resumes and hired 5,042 new employees. Two percent of the people that submitted resumes were hired. The American Psychotherapy Club research reveals that two percent of the general population is crazy...coincidence? I think not!

My unreliable sources indicate that, in the early seventies, Southwest Airlines developed a proactive and humorous program that was designed to improve Southwest employee morale and productivity while reducing turnover. Their theory was based on the concept that morale, output and retention are high when employees are having fun. The original program was coded LUV. Sources point out that the code name stood for "Liven Up our Visitors." From check-in to boarding, excitable passengers were identified as ideal

Irma: The expert in customer service

Here Irma is "training" a new bartender on the importance of customer service. She was a real stickler for detail and expected a "full" shot of whiskey in her glass. You can bet she got a full-glass shot next round of drinks.

candidates for employee entertainment. The LUV training taught employees how to identify over-exuberant situations, laughing at those customers who demand special consideration. Then the "fun" begins.

Other airline employees try to perform fun things to entertain the passengers. The secret at Southwest is to permit passengers to perform humorous antics to entertain the employees. Why do you think Southwest is referred to as the "Fun Airline?" Why do you think employee morale is so high at Southwest? The company trains its employees in the LUV method of exploiting bizarre situations, in which passengers are allowed to display their strange behaviors. They set the stage for all to perform to the level of their abilities. So who is actually having all the fun?

Southwest television commercials, magazine ads and posters usually show people in humorous situations—highly entertaining for their employees! Next time you see one of these ads, take a close look at what is really being advertised! Weren't you really laughing at yourself?

The LUV training school teaches new employees to enjoy this unique entertainment in three critical areas of customer service: 1) Seat assignments (ha, ha); 2) Boarding (moo, moo); and 3); Seating (what, me move?). To enhance the entertainment value, a well-trained employee is coached in the three R's—Ridiculous, Radical and Rambunctious.

Caution. Rest assured, they have learned their lessons well!

Arguably, Southwest has the best customer service in the airline industry. It's time now, though, to turn the tables on those zany Southwest employees. It's time you have a chance to laugh at fellow passengers. Go it alone, who needs to be LUVed? You can be in the driver's (aisle or window) seat. You can chuckle while others curse. You can be in control. Get to the front of the line. Sit in the seat you want. Get more peanuts than anyone else. Get free drinks. Your next trip will be all about numero uno!

This manual reveals the secrets Southwest employees are prevented from sharing with the traveling public. The threat of demotion for violating the "Oath of Herb" dangles over the head of every employee should they reveal the truth about their LUV training. They will soon realize that my exhaustive research (Irma told me) reveals the untold truth. Quotes at the end of each section provide evidence that the amazing revelations in this manual are theoretically possible.

Southwest Airlines claims to be the "fun" airline, so let's see if they can take it as well as they dish it out! Just because we do some dumb things doesn't mean they should laugh at us. As passengers, let's show them our kind of LUV; some crazy LUV!

Spirit of Irma

Listen up,

"LUV, peanuts, crazy people, whatever! Here's the bottom line, if you've been paying attention, every red-blooded American loves a deal that saves 'em a buck. Here's an airline that doesn't cut into my liquor money. Gotta git to LA tomorrow? They'll gitcha there fast, cheap and on time. Ya got yerself a winner here!"

Lots' a Luck,

Irma

"SOUTHWEST AIRLINES HAS ONE OF THE MOST LOYAL WORKFORCES ON EARTH, AND THE REASON IS SO SIMPLE, MOST PEOPLE CAN'T FIGURE IT OUT,' SAYS COLLEEN BARRETT, PRESIDENT OF SOUTHWEST AIRLINES."

—*SOLUTIONS MAGAZINE*, WINTER 2002

Who Is Southwest Airlines?

You want an assigned what?

IF YOU ARE NOT FAMILIAR with Southwest Airlines, you'll need a little background to understand the bizarre revelations that will be divulged in the following chapters. Southwest is not your typical airline.

Like other airlines they have planes, you buy a ticket, wait in line, check-in your bag, wait in line, board, wait in line. Nevertheless, the similarities end with the typical airline's way of doing business and begin with the unique conduct of Southwest employees. Oh, yeah, First Class seating and in-flight meals—forget it! (See Chapter 2 on how to prepare for battle.)

They ask you to check-in at the gate an hour before your flight leaves. Once you reach the gate, you may have to wait in line if you weren't smart enough to check-in by means of the speedier methods Southwest offers. Passengers are not just checking in, they are essentially jockeying for position to get the best seat. Seats are "assigned" (ha, ha) on a first-come–first-seated basis. If you are first in line, you get a card with a big letter A.

Caution If you are last in line, you get a card with the letter C, which doesn't fill you with LUV, because you can bet a letter C seat wouldn't make your momma proud.

Like so many things in life, location is very important! Either you come early for a front line position or you use some dirty, sneaky, conniving technique to advance to the front. (See Chapter 3 for Line Advancement techniques.)

Once you have been assigned a letter, you now wait for the usual, not sure when, boarding call (remember—seats are not assigned). As the plane pulls up to the gate, the game begins. The gate gal proudly announces to anxiously waiting passengers, "For your convenience Southwest offers "OPEN" seating." Yes, it's a wide open boarding

Irma checks her bags, takes the seat she wants

Irma was always firm, but fair with people. Here she was told she may only check-in three bags. After thirty minutes of the "I Don't Think So Technique," she had no difficulty checking in all fifteen bags.

free for all, but passenger antics create very little
convenience for one another. OPEN is another
one of those secret company code words employees learned in their LUV passenger training.
Employees enjoy this one, because they know it
stands for "**O**nly the **P**ushy **E**nter **N**ow."

Southwest pioneered the OPEN seating mad
rush with the theory that, "We created a *level
playing field*, so let them fight it out." If you assign
seats like everyone else, there's little desire for
passengers to perform. This way, the pressure for
a good seat starts the day the ticket is bought. The
theory supports the employee entertainment program, as passengers are in the competitive spirit
before they ever get to the airport. By the time
they get to the gate, they are pumped! Even the
last person to make a reservation (and probably
pays more) can battle fairly for a good seat. The
system insures a lively group because everyone
gets to play. The thrill of victory pulsates through
passenger veins!

I won't even dignify the pre-boarding process.
I find the topic irritating, primarily because you
can be in the "A group," yet eighty, quite healthy
looking pre-boards are lined up ahead of you.
(Look somewhere in Chapter 4).

Now, having an A card doesn't mean you get
on first. It means you get to board with the first
group of 40 or so people. Following the boarding
announcement, cardholders sprint to the gate to

secure front positions. The "boarding" (moo, moo) continues with the B, then finally the C group, until all the cattle have been herded on board. It is important to know that it is possible to be in the A group and be the forty-fifth passenger to board or be in the B group and be the forty-sixth to board. (See Chapter 4 for Herd Advancement techniques.)

Okay, finally you are lined up in the jetway, waiting to board, hoping to get a good seat. But wait! What about the all the carry-on junk you are taking to Grandma's house? What if there is no overhead bin space left? Oh, man, it's always something! (See Chapter 5 for Overhead Techniques For Swine.)

Bags are stowed, now to find a seat. If you were in the A group, you may choose from a selection of fine seating. If you hit the C group, you probably get your choice of middle and restroom area seats. In any case, the game doesn't end merely because you got the seat you want.

Being in the A or B group, you may have choice "seating" (what, me move?), but will someone be sitting next to you? As people parade down the aisle, they scope out their final resting place. You must protect your area! You don't want anyone sitting next to you. If the plane is one person short of full – that open seat belongs next to you! You can create your own First Class section. (See Chapter 6 for techniques in Seat and Row Management.)

You should have the seat, space and comfort you deserve. But what happens when the flight is full and you have no place to rest your arms? How uncivilized! You are entitled to the entire armrest, both of them! (See Chapter 7 for the rules of Elbow Etiquette.)

Southwest Airlines is nuts! It's all about the Peanut. The nut that made Southwest famous. The true power of the peanut is revealed. (See Chapter 8 to learn Mind Control).

Like every other airline, when all have been seated, the plane eventually takes off. But on Southwest, there are no meals, unless you consider peanuts and orange fish-shaped things fine dining. The soda is free, but a cold stiff one costs you. For the price of a ticket, you deserve all the free drinks, peanuts and fishies you want. (See Chapter 9 for Flight Attendant Manipulation techniques to get all the free stuff you want.)

In summary, here is the passenger war game! Move up in the check-in line, get on board early to get the seat you deserve. Keep the seats next to you unoccupied so you can stretch out and enjoy the flight. Then sit back and have a cold one on Southwest.

Having enjoyed a first-class flight is not to imply that you have successfully beat the system. Not only do you have to get the seat and service you want, but you must also exit the plane on your terms, as well. (See Chapter 10 to move the slugs along their merry way.)

You will not be the only passenger that has learned these unique travel skills. There is some top-notch talent out there, so you'll need to discipline yourself, work hard and practice diligently. This flight manual is the result of watching and learning from the best performers in the business. (See Chapter 11 to enjoy the exploits of your fellow passengers.)

Finally, once you have gained boarding expertise, you will want the recognition you have rightfully earned. Your status as a boarding specialist needs to be documented. Flash your card and watch passengers and employees alike back off and give you room to operate. (See Chapter 12 to get your designation.)

Remember, there are those who will work against you. If you use the techniques properly, passengers cannot gain an advantage over you; employees will not laugh at you. "Battle the Cattle" and win the game!

 **Note** If you end up in the C group, maybe you did not practice your techniques. Or, as you can see from the quote below, they want all passengers to be C's, because the company's first concern is employee entertainment.

Listen up,

"You want an assigned seat? Commit murder in
Texas! Myself, I get the seat I want, where I
want and when I want! Don't just stand there
bellyachin. Git down and shut up! Americans love
the freedom of choice. Go ahead and choose, but
don't tread on me! This is the only airline that
doesn't whine at me about sittin in a seat some
dummy picked for me. I ain't in first grade.
Nobody "assigns" me a seat!

Lots' a Luck,

Irma

"WE CALL OUR PASSENGERS CUSTOMERS WITH A CAPITAL C, BUT WE ALSO
SAY THAT OUR EMPLOYEES ARE OUR FIRST CUSTOMER."

—SOLUTIONS MAGAZINE, WINTER 2002
QUOTE BY COLLEEN BARRETT, PRESIDENT SOUTHWEST AIRLINES

Warming Up for the Battle

This is no place for wimps!

You're sitting on the bed next to your suitcase, eyes glazed over, staring out the window. You know what's ahead of you for the next six hours. Like the pre-game tension athletes experience, you feel nervous, tense and excited. You look forward to seeing Mother, but thinking about the usual flight routine gives you heartburn.

As you grab your bags and walk to the car, you reach in your pocket to double-check the departure time. Yup, same time, flight and terminal as when you checked an hour ago. It's Southwest

flight 293 to beautiful Boise, and you know you
have to get to the airport at just the right time to
get a good seat. A good seat, that is, if you are
among the first to board. You know full well that
other passengers also want prime seating. You feel
tingly all over, knowing you have to beat the
bunch to the punch!

Driving to the shuttle parking lot, you are
watching for cars heading to the airport. Are they
on a Southwest flight? You see jets rising into the
sky as you pull into the lot. While looking for a
parking spot, a loaded shuttle passes you, bound
for the airport. Could that entire van full of people be on the same flight? Your stomach churns as
you imagine every shuttle that drives by destined
for flight 293. Did you leave early enough? Will
you be in the last group when you finally get to
the gate? You park your car and plop your head
on the steering wheel, wallowing in self-despair.

By the time the shuttle pulls up to your car,
you have talked yourself into a respectable level of
self-confidence. You are now poised. You realize
that you are good; a pro. You can handle the pressure. You can get the seat you want. You will win.
When the driver is done tossing your luggage in
the van, you boldly stride up the steps and secure
a front row seat. Your palms are sweaty and you
rock back and forth in anticipation of the loom-
ing battle. The violent motion of the van cutting
off cars and the driver forcing his way into openings that don't exist stimulates your adrenalin

Irma delighted in a good battle

Irma demonstrates the correct method of applying the "Shoulder Jamb Technique" to force unmanageable luggage into her vehicle. So, maybe she had a teeny bit of a temper!

flow. Bouncing up and down in unison, you are as one with the shuttle.

When the driver growls, "Which terminal ya want, Mack?" you feel the competitive spirit surging through your body.

You fire back, "Southwest, curb-side and move it!"

The shuttle screeches to a halt, in fairly close proximity to the skycap counter. The driver limps down the steps and heaves your bags onto the sidewalk. Slowly and confidently, you glide out of the van, as does a true champion. It's time to go for it! A reluctant tip to the driver in appreciation for the abuse, and you look up to face the first event in your travel marathon.

Grabbing what's left of your bags, you can't help but feel like the sheriff at the OK Corral.

Caution Guns loaded, attitude bad! Today, somebody is gonna pay!

You are going to have it out with many lines of passengers today, but as you inhale the gentle breeze of carbon monoxide, you turn green at the fleeting thought of losing even one battle. Each battle in the war is a victory in the making. Think positive!

While waiting in line, you immediately begin to size up the competition. Who else is going to Boise? You need an advantage. As you inch forward, optional plans of attack race through your mind. You peek over shoulders, scope out luggage destination tags and eavesdrop on conversations to learn who else is Boise-bound. You seek the enemy.

As luggage is tossed from incoming shuttles in front of your position, that initial surge of hostility jolts your world. Are passengers pulling their luggage toward the front of the line, attempting to take advantage of you? No, wait; they are actually walking toward the end of the line. As they move along the line, you push your luggage in front of you and turn sideways to block their ability to cut into your spot. Your blood flows hot, your stare grows cold. You are pumped as the first action of the day begins. The beginning volley has been shot. You feel a sense of joy with your first success, as no one has been able to advance in front of you.

When the skycap gets close, you whip out your ticket and ID, whispering quietly so others can't hear, "I'm going to Boise." When the skycap tags your bag, you stand such that nobody in line can see your destination. You tip the skycap enough to make sure your bag isn't damaged or doesn't end up in Cleveland, then hit the terminal door running. Stage one is complete, mission accomplished.

That was a nice start; now for the real game. In technical terms, you have just completed the "pre-flight rage" warm-up. This is significant, mentally, as you are now in a truly competitive state of mind. Heading toward the gate, visions of stretching out in a first-rate seat dance through your head. As you pass others on their way to the gate, you can sense that none of them know that First Class seating is actually available on Southwest. But you know First Class seating can be had, and it feels good to be a winner. You're feeling in top form. You can taste the peanuts!

As you approach the security checkpoint, you stop and take a deep breath. A confident smile broadens across your face. You don't worry about what others may think. You are calming your racing heart, seeking focus and releasing negative energies. You are in control and about to enter the Zen-like state of a boarding expert.

 **Note** While in this cosmic zone, you are unbeatable. All you desire will be yours, on your terms.

Take What You Deserve

Has this been your experience? Do you feel confident, heading to the gate, that you will enjoy the customer service you deserve? Do you know how to *take* the service you expect and laugh at those that don't? If not, you are a wimp and you'd better get with the program! Come on; let's have some fun!

Spirit of Irma

Listen up,

"One thing you can count on, Americans love a good, clean, face to face confrontation. I enjoy the thrill of victory, the joy of competition. In the airline game, you take control; segment and domi- nate the competition. When I fly this airline I get goose bumps thinkin about segmenting some lolly- gagger from his front line position. Hostile pres- sure, relentlessly applied is my game!"

Lots' a Luck,

Irma

"MAYBE THEY'RE LAUGHING TO KEEP FROM CRYING," SAYS ED STEWART, A SPOKESMAN FOR SOUTHWEST AIRLINES.

—SOUTHWEST AIRLINES
OCTOBER 22, 2002

chapter

3

Line Advancement Techniques

*OPEN seating, offered for
whose convenience?*

OKAY, YOUR FLIGHT LEAVES AT 2:00 PM; it's 1:37 pm, and you didn't make the gate an hour before the flight time. What's your problem? Was it the overloaded shuttle bus, curbside security, terminal security, baggage security or just the security security? Perhaps you lost your identification, had to take your shoes off so you didn't beep or had to pull the lethal PC from your fifty-pound bag. Southwest may check-in fast with all their new-fangled improvements, but it's up to *you* to get to the gate on time!

The security line is long and passengers are watching carefully, awaiting the opportunity to hurriedly dart to the shortest line. As you approach the rear end of the longest line, you are terrified at the thought of being the last one on board. You'll probably end up helping the caterer load those little snack baskets.

You've got to move up in the security line; but more importantly, you have got to find a way to move up in the check-in line when you get to the gate! As an experienced Southwest Airlines travel veteran, I have developed tried-and-true techniques that you can use to advance in the check-in line, hold your position and get the best seat. In this chapter, you will learn the true A, B, C's of flying Southwest. Study the techniques well and you will get an A (card).

Line Advancement Techniques

With the new kiosk and curbside check-in, Southwest has done an admirable job of reducing the line at the gate. But, at some point, you may face the prospect of waiting in line. It may be your own fault, but you still want that A card! If you are the type that frequently runs late, I'll give you a little help. The following techniques have been developed and tested as sure-fire ways to move up in any line.

It's quite acceptable to look stupid! Displaying the right appearance and attitude can assure excellent results in the line advancement techniques. It's all in the way you are perceived! A look of stupidity and confusion throughout the game projects the appearance of innocent sincerity. The airline people are suckers for it! Your success depends on how cleverly you don't appear to be doing what you are about to do.

New Gate Technique

You are standing at Gate 9. If you are sincere, you can talk the airport announcement operator into announcing that the flight scheduled to go out on Gate 9 is now departing from Gate 75. You move up easily on this one, especially if you loudly proclaim, "Run like hell if you want a decent seat!"

Counter Technique

If the line is long and the agent is not yet behind the counter, consider standing behind the counter. When the agent arrives, ask a stupid question, and then give her your ticket as if you were the first one there. Offer to be of assistance; appear happy and helpful.

Employee Technique

A solid veteran keeps Southwest outerwear pieces readily available. Donning a Southwest sweatshirt gives you privileges. Move immediately and confidently to the very front of the line. Indicate to others that you are traveling on an employee ticket and may have to work. Good one!

 **Note** If you forget, you can always apply for a credit card and get a free tee shirt.

Count and Lie Technique

Always count the number of people in front of you. If you are only a person or two from getting in the A boarding group, you need to act. Walk forward to the first grandma type you see. Give her a big hug and holler, "Aunt Emma, how have you been? I didn't know you were on this flight." When she looks at you like you are crazy, start apologizing and talking, but stay in your new position. Who would yell at Auntie Em?

Tango Line Technique

This works great when the line is straight and you are late. Line up behind the last person at 90-degree angle to the line. People will naturally line up behind you. When the agent hollers at everyone to straighten out the line, sneak up a few positions in all the confusion. If you are bored, you can do the Tango Line to create a terminal snake.

Cart Technique

The transport cart is another good one. Tell the driver you are disabled (a big tip usually eliminates any questions) and to drive you to the gate. When he sets your carry-on by the counter, limp up to the first position. Others will be too embarrassed to challenge you.

My Friend Technique

It's a freebie anytime you have a friend lined up in front of you. Run up to her, waving and smiling, hug if you can. Everyone in line will be happy for you and would never make a fuss at the sight of a friendly reunion.

Motherhood Technique

Another freebie is a mother with children. Always watch for a child taking off from the mother (and they always do). Help herd the kid back in line, and then offer her your expert child-care assistance. You can move up in the line, because no one would ever challenge helping a mother. If it's really your day, you may get to pre-board with the family.

Piggyback Technique

A true veteran is always aware there are other seasoned pros that also know the game. When another works one of the line techniques, point it out to those in line, then loudly volunteer to go talk to the line skipper. When you do, give the person your regards, then turn to the others and proclaim, "It's okay, he was here before." Your boldness will be admired and you may stay in the position without fear of passenger retaliation.

Mad Cow Technique

No matter how long the check-in line is, approach the counter coughing and gagging—be convincing. Move to the front of the line. Tell the counter guy you have a rare, contagious disease (make up a name if they ask) and must sit in front so as not to infect others on the plane. Good odds on this one. Usually the people in line support the move.

SOB Technique

If you can ignore icy stares and crude comments just pick out your desired spot in line and settle in. Done with great success when you project the attitude that you are entitled to the spot.

Illegal Visitor Technique

If, for example, you are at Gate 9 call the airport announcement operator and ask to give the following announcement, "Mr. Jones from the INS, please report to Gate 9." The technique shortens the line considerably. This one works!

Irma always got to the front of the line

Irma was never too embarrassed to use the "Thug Technique." Throwing her weight around to force her way in line was just part of her unique charm. Her confidence and class were an inspiration to us all.

Correct Line Technique

As you approach the end of the line, ask the person in front of you if this is the check-in for Cleveland. You know it's for Tampa, but insist it's for Cleveland. Then, in a confused fashion, move up the line asking others until you have found someone as confused as you appear. Walk with the guy toward the counter. When you both agree the line is for Tampa, return with him to an advanced line position. Compliment the guy regarding his intelligence. Others will still be asking if they are in the correct line.

Embarrassed Technique

When at the back of the line, wave the pair of underwear you always keep in your briefcase and shout to your victim, "Hey, you forgot these!" When the person comes back to see what you want, he will undoubtedly ask you if you are crazy; those aren't his underwear. Walk back with him to his position near the front of the line, apologizing. Others will be so embarrassed for the person they will not say a word to you about your advancement.

Courteous Technique

Walk up to the guy in the front of the line and ask him to hold your ticket, you'll be right back. Upon your return, thank him as he returns your ticket and continue with small talk. Others will think you belong in the line and just went to the bathroom.

Chain Gang Technique

Just before you get to the gate, you and your travel companion put on the handcuffs you always carry in your bag. Take your "prisoner" to the front of the line, lean on the counter and look mean. If the lady behind you makes a comment, just turn and say, "Sorry Ma'am, this is official business."

 **Caution** Be careful not to let the check-in gal see the handcuffs or they won't let you on.

Inner Conflict Technique

No matter where you are in the line, this one will advance you quite nicely. With a pained look, ask the guy in front of you if he heard voices. Before he can respond, smack your forehead and mumble, "You again, stop it, go away, shut up!" Appear confused, advance in the line and then do it again to the next person in front of you. Everyone will step back and allow you to move up without a challenge.

Got Guts Technique

Always carry a yellow cloth covering that will fit nicely over your carry-on. The covering should have a label on it that reads, "HUMAN ORGANS—KEEP STERILE." It's worth the effort; people will back away as you operate at the head of the line. If questioned, merely indicate that you must have an aisle seat, in case the container leaks.

Duck and Delay Technique

The "Duck and Delay" is an employee technique learned in the LUV training. Just before they announce the delay of a flight, Southwest employees often duck behind the counter to hide. This is advantageous for the wily veteran stuck at the end of the line. Walk up and lean over the counter, wave your arms violently so other passengers think you are giving the counter gal genuine hell. People like that! Ask the gal behind the counter if she would like coffee, donuts or if there is anything you can do. When she thanks you, indicate that you will be nearby so she can alert you when the line is ready to form again. Stay in front; after all, you are a hero.

These are the basic techniques. Do not try to develop your own until you have mastered these fundamental skills. Once you have gained expertise and confidence in your new abilities, you can lead any line you choose!

In summary, get that A card, be on the plane first and secure the ideal seating environment. Failure to gain a lead position in the check-in line is not a good start, but it does not mean you lose the game. The only way you can lose is to feel guilty for using your skills. Failing to cut ahead of that little old lady because you feel guilty will only get you a middle seat in the toilet section. The skilled Southwest traveler knows the techniques, never whining, backing off or giving in because of a guilty conscience.

The concept of not assigning seats appears a bit inconvenient, perhaps barbaric. With assigned seating, we as consumers feel that, regardless of the many airport hassles, eventually our own seat is waiting for us. If you've flown a few other airlines, you know that is a bunch of bull! On numerous occasions, I have tried to get round-trip seat assignments and have been told seats will be assigned when I check in. Now there is a crapshoot if I've ever seen one. I get a middle seat at check-in, greeted at the gate with an oversold announcement, and then asked if I am willing to give up my seat for $100. Of course, the $100 is in ticket vouchers for the same airline that's sending me on the next flight home to Los Angeles via Atlanta.

At least on Southwest, you get a fighting chance. There are no promises, no seat assignments and no favorites. I'll take my chances on getting a good seat, based on my ability to use the techniques in this manual. Don't fill me full of crap; all I want is a fair shot. Give me an equal opportunity and I will be accountable for my own seat assignment.

Listen up,

"You enjoy waiting in line? Join the Army! Hurry up and wait! Americans get aggravated when they have to wait in line. I always bring my pet with me, just in case some dang line ain't movin. My pet "Wild Turkey®", that is. About eight to ten slugs, and we're flyin through any line! All these new-fangled line-reducing gadgets they got on this here airline have clipped my wings a tad!"

Lots' a Luck

Irma

"I OFTEN HEAR FROM CUSTOMERS WHO TELL ME: 'SOUTHWEST AIRLINES IS GREAT, EXCEPT FOR THE FACT THAT YOU DON'T ASSIGN SEATS. SINCE ALMOST ALL OTHER AIRLINES OFFER THIS AMENITY, SOUTHWEST IS CONSPICUOUS BY OUR ABSTENTION."

—COLLEEN BARRETT
PRESIDENT AND CHIEF OPERATING OFFICER
SOUTHWEST AIRLINES SPIRIT
OCTOBER 2001

Herd Advancement Techniques

It's all about line position, move it!

ONCE YOU GET YOUR GRADE CARD (boarding pass), preparation for boarding begins and you enter into the next series of advancement techniques. Of course, if you are clever enough to get in the pre-board group, you automatically get an A+.

Regardless of the boarding card letter you have in your hand, when the call to board is given, you will be caught up in the "herd" mentality. Manners, courtesy and respect go out the door. Pushing, shoving and jostling replace common sense. Like cattle moving toward water, nothing, and no one stands in your way. You cannot be a cow(ard); bull your way to the front!

Managing the herd is the most difficult of the seating challenges. This is where the bold, wily, crafty veteran shines. She tramples through the herd, secures her position and ultimately controls her boarding experience. Above all, her enthusiasm to carry out her well-honed techniques is never dampened by the cold, icy stares of losers.

Check Your Angle

You have your boarding card, but you still need to gain an edge in line position. While sitting in the boarding lounge area, before the call to board, it is imperative you are seated strategically. Seat yourself such that when the group boarding line begins to form you have the proper "angle of intrusion." The proper angle, adjacent to the line, is critical if you are going to cut off those in front of you, giving the appearance it is their fault. A forty-five degree angle to the line provides an unbeatable advantage.

 **Note** Have your carry-on at the same angle as your body position.

As the line forms and starts to move forward, make your move. Take a long stride at the correct angle, stay low, and knife your way into the line. You should be able to advance three to four positions from your starting point. Be disciplined in the angle of approach and stay low to avoid flying elbows. You are a pro if this is accomplished and the guy you cut off drops his newspaper to apologize.

Herd Gathering (Boarding Position) Techniques

Boarding line maneuvers require a bold and aggressive attitude. Opportunities open and close in a matter of seconds. The quick-thinking and creative passenger never misses a chance. The techniques that follow have proven successful over the years. Have the confidence to give them a try! Don't take a middle seat to anyone.

There are two skills rookies need to master. First, is the pre-board line. Techniques in pre-board require creativity, daring and a total lack of coordination. The other is the general boarding line. To be successful here, you must be cunning and agile with graceful maneuverability.

Pre-Board Specials

Pre-board assignment logic is among the greatest mysteries in the airline industry. Airlines say pre-boarding is for disabled, those who need assistance and parents with small children. If you watch the majority of people in pre-board, you know that is a bunch of baloney! Aero Plane Magazine states that "ninety-six percent of pre-boards are no more disabled than the rest of the herd." Few need assistance, most of the kids can walk, and it doesn't take five people to carry a baby!

When it comes to pre-boarding, those with a conscience lose! Southwest gives a little blue "pre-board card" to those who ask. There are other ways to pre-board. Here are a few particularly disgusting ways to pre-board while others grumble.

Wheel Me Technique
If you see a wheelchair sitting empty by the wall, jump in when no one is looking. Don't worry about a pre-board card; just tell them you were too disabled to ask for one. If they press you, suggest that you could have been discriminated against when you checked in, but you are not sure. Before you can finish, they will wheel you on.

Irma was a wheeler and dealer

Irma demonstrates one of her favorite techniques; one she developed to an art form. She called this the "Whip and Wheel Technique." The woman was fearless! When she was in a hurry to get to the front of the line, bodies went flying. Oh, you think Security would stop her? They don't get paid enough.

5th Wheel Technique

As you walk to the gate, you see an older lady in the pre-board area, sitting in a wheel chair. Be kind. Walk over and start a long discussion—until the pre-board call. Then walk on behind the wheel chair. If they ask, just tell them you want to be with your dear, sweet grandma. How could they stop you? We all have a grandma.

Bad Wheel Technique

Seasoned travelers always carry a folding cane or at least an elastic bandage, in case of a "sudden" injury. Works every time.

Useless Dad Technique

Here is a beauty. Poor woman struggling with two little kids. Be polite and truly offer assistance. Carry her luggage, diaper bag, etc. Or, if you are too shy to offer mom some help, just stand close by, following her on. Act like a useless father. Either way you are on!

Dumb Dad Technique

Wait until a mother with children in pre-board enter the jet way, then run through the area, asking the gate gal if she already let your wife and kids on. They won't say a word because they feel sorry for what is waiting for you.

Note The same technique can be used with a wheelchair person.

Flying Mac Technique

If you are carrying food on the plane with you, tell the gate attendant you are delivering the pilot's McDonald's order. Fifty–fifty chance on this one.

Helping Hand Technique

Suppose you have a disabled friend or a veteran traveler with a folding cane; don't be afraid to offer her an arm for assistance. Who would stop a caring friend?

Caution If she is faking, be sure not to blow her cover.

Sad Sack Technique

Stand in the boarding line with a pained look or even a few tears (for a real pained look, just think about having to sit next to the lady with two kids). You may get a soft gate agent to buy it and let you on. Works easier if you gag and cough a little bit.

Dumb Jock Technique

As the gate gal is calling for pre-boards, walk up to her slowly and ask if she can help you down the jet way, because of your old football injury. Works best if you have a nice body and a dumb look on your face.

Dumb Doc Technique

High percentage and takes guts, but I've seen it work. If you are really late (back of the C group) proceed quickly from check-in to the pre-board area. Walk past other pre-boards; with a look of panic, ask the gate guy if he took a wheelchair on board yet. When he says yes, act disgusted, telling him you gave instructions to wait until you returned to attend your patient. This one gets you on right away.

The General Boarding Line (Ordering the Herd)

Southwest employees find the boarding process the most entertaining of all the customer shows. Their boss calls it "a ballet of motion." The rest of us think of it as the "running of the bulls." They gather behind the counter to rate the creativity of passenger boarding techniques. For real fun, they might announce a delay or give a severe weather update. These are sick people!

But you can beat them at their own game. You can gain an advantage over fellow passengers. What follows are the best of the veteran traveler boarding techniques.

 **Caution** No rookie stuff here!

The number one advantage is to be in the first position in the A stall, ready to board. At the very least, be near the front of your boarding group. On the other hand, that's no fun! So, if you are stuck at the end of the boarding line use one of the sophisticated techniques that follow to move on up.

Poor Dummy Technique

Wear your most confused look. Ask questions that have no answers, such as, "If the plane doesn't show up, will it be on time?" Inch forward and twist in between people. If you get between two people traveling together, apologize and step backwards toward the gate. Remember, confusion and weirdness give you an advantage over other passengers, as well as airline employees.

Herb Technique

Regardless of your letter assignment, go right to the front of the A group, as if you're entitled to be first. When the gate guy sees you have a C card, tell him uncle Herb said for you to board immediately! Success on this one depends on whether or not the gate guy is a brown-nosing company man.

Pick and Roll Technique

When traveling with a partner, work together. If you both are at the back of the line, have your partner turn into the group while you step up and advance your position. Alternate and continue to pick and roll until you have reached the front of the line. Go slowly, though, it's not the NBA.

The "B Group" Slide Technique

Even though you have a B card, line up with the cattle in the A group. When the gate guy says you should be in the B group, tell him you thought B was to follow A. Be sincere, act confused. He will tell you to line up in the B stall. Apologize, smile and slide in the front position of the B group. Be humble.

Nice Guy Technique

If you want to be fairly honest, and you have no guts, you could offer a $10 bill for a front line position. Works well on accountants and little old ladies heading for Las Vegas.

Too New Technique

Sometimes you can fool a new traveler by telling her how badly you feel for her because she is first in the A group line. The first group has to sit in the "dangerous front position" of the plane. Tell her the back of the plane is safer than the front, but you'll trade with her because she is a rookie traveler and you want to assure her safety.

 **Note** As she walks past you in your front row aisle seat, cover your face.

Step and Slide Technique

While waiting in line, always stand with legs spread wide and carry-ons in front of your feet. This takes up a lot of room and annoys others. Pick up your carry-ons and step into open areas, sliding forward as many positions as you can. Continue until you have the lead position. Be smooth and oh, so cheery.

Elbow and Turn Technique

When you are next to another passenger and can't seem to get ahead, turn and back into him, getting as close as possible. Put your hand on your hip, elbow out and in front of your competition. Stepping toward the gate, turn into the person and advance your position. Remember, people do not like contact; take advantage of that weakness.

Money Technique

Turn back and forth furiously, staring at the floor. Exclaim loudly, "Did anyone find the bundle of $20 bills I dropped?" As others help you look, bend over and back toward the gate. During the confusion, you will easily advance your position. People will give you room. No one likes a butt check.

Ceiling Technique

If the $20 bill trick doesn't work, try this one. When you are waiting in line with what appears to be a group of rookie travelers, stand with hands on hips and stare up at the ceiling. Occasionally, point to the ceiling with a confused look, asking yourself aloud, "Was sup der?" Continue looking up. As others look up, use the Elbow and Turn Technique. Confused weirdness really works.

Belch and Roll Technique
The ability to produce a good loud belch on command can be a useful boarding and seating skill. No matter where you are in the line, produce the loudest belch you can bring up, followed by a mumbling apology. Gradually move forward as others back away from you. The key is to mumble the apology louder each time you advance.

Bag and Turn Technique
Like the Elbow and Turn Technique; the bag can be used as an advancement weapon. A large shoulder bag works quite nicely. Move into the group, leading with the bag. Each time you are stopped, position your bag into one of the herd, turn and step forward. Some people get a little irritated with this one. Use this to your advantage. Turn back to apologize, backing into the person in front of you. Repeat and continue to advance. Turn a negative into a positive move forward. Good one.

Donation Technique
Regardless of the group you are in, move from the end of the line to the front, asking for donations. People will back away and avoid you as you extend your open cap. When you get to the front of the line, ask the gate gal if she would like to make a donation. While she looks away, plant

yourself in front of the line. You will not be both-
ered for the rest of the flight.

Name Dropper Technique

If you don't know the name of the gate gal, go
back to the counter and ask if Jim is at the gate
today. When they inform you, "Mary is at the
gate today," run to the gate asking for Mary. Walk
through the line calling her name. When you get
to the front of the line say loudly, "Mary is the
flight on time?" Regardless of her answer, stay at
the front of the line. No one will say anything
because they think Mary is your good friend.

Gimme Room Technique

If you are first in line and want some space to
breathe or just feel like having a little fun, try this
one. Turn and face the group with your bag in
front of you, at your feet. Fold your arms across
your chest and stare straight into the line. This
one is always good for five feet of open space.

Girl Scout Technique

During Girl Scout Cookie season, be sure to buy a
couple of boxes and have them handy when you
get in line. No hurry to get in line, because this
one will move you forward. Hold up the cookies
and advance in the line, asking each person if

they want to support the Girl Scouts. When you finally get to the front, turn and face the group. They will look the other way and give you plenty of extra room.

Several airports around the country have taken some of the art form out of the boarding process, having installed group-herding stations. They call them "boarding lanes." I like to think of them as "passing lanes." The separation of the A, B, and C groups with partitions should not hinder the use of these boarding techniques. As a matter of fact, it neatly segments the competition. Let' em make it tougher; the creative boarding specialist always enjoys a good challenge.

An airline employee, impressed with your work, will give you a break simply because you have demonstrated creativity and style in your techniques. As was emphasized before, the employees are truly entertained by the antics of the passengers. Show them your best stuff, be stylish and throw in an occasional combination of techniques. You will be laughing while they're wondering. Give them something to talk about at coffee break.

Spirit of Irma

Listen up,

"We're talking here about an airline that's taken the boredom out of boarding. Wild-eyed passengers, wired for fun, in the hunt for their perfect seating arrangement. Tasting the thrill of victory when they secure their desired location. The only kick better than the emotional high of taking the seat I want, is killing the taste of their free sody pop with a shot or two of Wild Turkey®!"

Lots' a Luck,

Irma

" SOUTHWEST HAS DEVELOPED THE CONCEPT OF THE QUICK TURN INTO AN ART, AND OUR EMPLOYEES AND OUR CUSTOMERS PARTICIPATE IN A BALLET OF MOTION EACH TIME WE LOAD AND UNLOAD AN AIRCRAFT."

—COLLEEN BARRETT
PRESIDENT AND CHIEF OPERATING OFFICER
SOUTHWEST AIRLINES SPIRIT
OCTOBER 2001

chapter

5

Overhead Bin Pig

Swine sounds so much classier!

I AM CONTINUALLY AMAZED TO SEE how many passengers board with the style of bags you'd see on a desert caravan. Who are these people? They seem so indignant when passengers get upset simply because they hog an entire overhead bin. I'm sure you have seen the tears of laughter in the eyes of flight attendants who painfully observe needless attacks on overhead compartments. It becomes immediately apparent that eye-hand coordination is not a carry-on requirement!

As a knowledgeable traveler, you know the carry-on-to-overhead fit ratio. Yet, when Grandma asks you to take home a 50-pound bag of oatmeal cookies, what can you do? Did you ever try to get three square feet of unnecessary stuff into a two square foot overhead space? How do you find overhead room for the classy new suit you bought with your Las Vegas winnings? It is your good fortune to have a section devoted to overhead bin storage.

The expert boarding specialist can be a *Bin Hog*, yet maintain an air of dignity. There is no reason for you to be inconvenienced by having to endure Grandma's cookies on your lap for the entire flight. You should never have to sit with your knees under your chin because you had to stuff your Elvis outfit under the seat in front of you. Customer service means all your junk is stored. Take command of the overhead!

Regardless of when you board, you can never enter the plane with a sense of accomplishment. Your work is not yet done. As you walk into the plane and turn down the aisle way, your keen sense of observation must be razor sharp. Simultaneously, you are viewing open seats, backs of heads, flight attendants and – overhead bin availability. Sometimes the order of priorities is overwhelming! Here are a few simple rules to assist your customer service efforts:

Rules of the Aisle

1. If you spot a good seat, throw your junk in the first open overhead space you find. Keep your elbows or butt in the aisle as you fill the bin so no one can pass you and steal your seat.

2. Always squeeze by the guy filling an overhead, which gives you a good shot at the seat he thought was his.

3. If you find a good seat and you have yet to find overhead space, throw your shirt, diaper, wig, cap, anything on the seat to save it, then apply the techniques that follow.

4. Always have your bag in front of you. As a weapon, it moves people along and intimidates the guy in front of you that just stole your bin spot.

5. Offer help to others; you might be able to squeeze your stuff in as well, or convince them their junk won't fit, so you can take the space.

6. If you actually are of some help to someone, be sure to sit close by; you may get free cookies or a drink for your assistance.

7. Open all closed bins as you walk down the aisle. That does two things. It slows up the line to gain additional planning time and many times brings help from an annoyed attendant.

The following section on techniques is designed to help those of you who have occasional storage needs, but don't want to appear piggish. Neither be it pig nor be it hog; the classy boarding specialist prefers—Swine! Whatever you are called, seize the space to which you are entitled.

 **Note** The attendants readily differentiate the pigs from the swine by their oinks!

Overhead Swine Techniques

Slide and Squash Technique

The overhead is full, except for a small area in front of a box. Move the box over in front of the bag full of glassware. Place your item in the newly created opening, and then slam the door shut. If any glass is broken, the guy pulling out his box will be blamed.

Coat Skrunch Technique

Any coat in the bin is asking to be wrinkled. Place your item in front of or on top of the coat and push to the back. This provides additional cushioning to protect your junk.

Irma got a kick out of filling an overhead bin

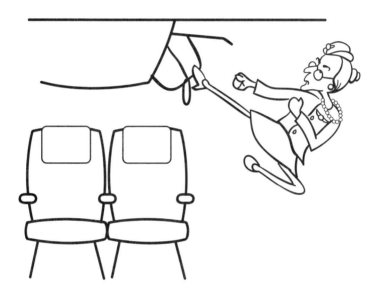

This advanced overhead technique is called the "Kung Fu Bin-Buster Technique." Irma was the only known boarding specialist to have ever performed this technique and not pull a groin muscle.

Whine and Cry Technique

If you cannot find overhead space, just open the door and push your bag in just enough so the weight is on the shelf. Then just stand there with that innocent, hurt, sulking look until an attendant takes pity on you. Then it's their problem.

Not My Problem Technique

If you get desperate, empty the overhead, place your items inside and then take your seat. Works great if you can dump the displaced items on an empty seat. It then becomes someone else's problem.

Coat Drop Technique

If you know the coats filling the bin belong to the person seated directly under the bin you can work this to your advantage. Shuffle the coats around, and then drop one or two on the owner. Apologize and stuff them back in the bin. After two or three times, the owner will usually grab and hold the coats. You get the space you wanted.

Neat Freak Technique

The bin is filled just enough so that you can't fit in your bag. As usual, everyone is watching. Slowly shift items around so it appears you are carefully rearranging the bin to fit your bag. Soon passengers will look away. In that moment, quickly force everything to one side and slam your bag in the new opening.

Caution Don't forget the happy face.

That's Mine Technique

Sometimes you can pull one over on a rookie traveler. Should you happen to be standing behind a rookie as she takes the last open spot in the bin, just remind her that the bin belongs to you, as your seat is just below the overhead. The bonus is that you intimidate her out of the seat, as well.

Body Bag Technique

You can see the lady in front of you will not leave enough room for both her stuff and your bag. As she starts to move her bag to the bin, quickly announce, "Oh good, that's lucky, I'll have just enough room for my 'HUMAN ORGANS' medical bag!" She will quickly move to another overhead. Great combination! Remember, you used the same bag to advance in line earlier!

Swine Slam Technique

Don't do like so many passengers do, that is, slam
the wide open door closed to get that extra squash
to force stuff in the bin. Instead, gently bring the
door down to a contact point with the bin con-
tents. Then, with a smile, use all your force to
mash the door shut for a perfect fit. That's the difference between a piggy hog and a classy swine!

For some strange reason, people get all bent
out of shape if they think their belongings might
get smashed up a bit. Always keep a sharp eye on
who is watching you. Smile and look concerned
about their stuff.

A few years ago, Southwest changed their
carry-on policy to a two bag per customer limit.
They put on a special customer awareness "Bin
Hog" campaign. The official day of the policy
change was Ground Hog Day. On that day only,
you could carry-on more than two bags if you
wore a pig nose and would oink down the jet way.
These people are crazy—and Herb says I'm nuts!

Spirit of Irma

Listen up,

"All this hog-wash talk about carry-on's makes me squeal. Americans pack for action, pack as much and whatever they want. Don't tell me what to pack and don't help me load the dang overhead. I'm no wimp! I don't need any of that loving help. Touch my bags and you will feel the sting of my American made maple-wood cane."

Lots' a Luck,

Irma

"DON'T BE A BIN HOG"

—*Southwest Poster*
Phoenix Airport

chapter 6

Save That Seat

Innovative seat selection and row maintenance.

Excellent work; you have successfully applied the techniques and secured a good seat. Great, but your work is still not yet done, as your ultimate goal is to establish your personal "comfort zone." Specifically, no one is sitting next to you. Room to spread out. Nobody to bug you.

Note Veteran travelers jealously guard the zone.

This is where the men are separated from the boys, women from the girls. The comfort of your flight rests on your ability to manage the zone. You have worked hard to board first so you could select the seat you desire. The row is empty, no one within an arm's length. Come hell or high water, you will own the entire row! You are now in the comfort zone. Your last concern is airline profitability!

Southwest does the passenger a favor by not assigning seats, from the standpoint that you get to sit wherever or next to whomever you want. The only downside is that that weirdo behind you in the boarding line seemed to like your smile and may choose to sit next to you. You want your space, your way!

Overzealous use of seat management techniques may be of concern to Southwest Airlines. They like systematic and orderly passenger seating.

 **Caution** So, by all means, conduct yourself (or at least give the appearance) of a gentleman or lady. Then, go for it!

On many flights you will hear the attendants announce, "Don't avoid eye contact, please take the first available seat." The truth is, if you want control of the entire row, stare 'em all down! Intimidated passengers will just walk on by.

Flight attendants have witnessed some of the gems that follow, but they could never imagine that passengers might someday have the complete book on seat management. It's all yours!

Seat Management Techniques

Imagine you are sitting alone, comfortable, and ready to take on all comers, never backing off from those who try to invade your territory! You are now in charge! The following techniques will secure the comfort zone you have established:

Bag & Gag Technique

Take the Barf Bag from behind the seat in front of you and hold over your mouth. As people move close to you or eye one of your seats, heave into the bag. Make your heaves moderately loud and serious. A veteran will make eye contact and give a teary, strained, whiny look. Good one!

 **Note** This is a good time to place the "plastic puke" you bought at the gag store on the seat next to you.

Zombie Stare Technique

Sit tall in the seat, eyes wide and staring straight ahead. From that position, bounce your head back against the headrest and forward to the seat in front of you. Continue until dizzy. Do not make eye contact with others. Throw in an occasional low grunting noise, and yer sittin' by yerself!

Angry Mother Technique

If a passenger asks if the middle or window seat is taken, tell them, "The middle seat is available. But, the window seat is being saved for my pregnant sister, who just took the diarrheic twin babies to the restroom." They will move to the back before you can say "dirty diapers."

Quiet, He's Asleep Technique

Grab a few pillows from the overhead and pile them on the seat next to you. Throw a blanket over the bottom half and a newspaper on top. Got a 50-50 chance, but you may get a free drink from the flight crew for creativity.

Busy Technique

Pull down all the trays on the seats in your row and put your computer, lunch, cell phone, briefcase, books, drinks and whatever on them. Act busy writing, calling or computing. If you are asked if those seats are taken, look up with impatient disgust.

Repair Technique

Pull the tray down in the seat next to you. Put a pencil just behind the tray hinge. If you are asked to raise the tray so the lady can get in, just tell her it won't move—must be broken.

 **Bonus Tip** Tell the flight attendant that the mechanic was just here and said not to move the tray until he gets back. Good success rate on this one.

Bad Baby Technique

If you have or can borrow a screaming baby, hold the child up as he is crying. Make sure everyone sees how embarrassed you are. If you don't have a baby, borrow a diaper and put it in the seat next to you (bonus if diaper is dirty). High percentage on getting the whole row.

Fetal Technique

Sit in the middle seat, assuming a fetal position with feet tucked underneath. Rock back and forth sucking your thumb and singing "98 Bottles of Beer on the Wall." Good for getting the whole row. Would you sit next to this guy?

Goat Herder Technique

I've seen it and smelled it, but I have never had
the guts to try it. Nevertheless, there are those
skilled travelers that know how to get things
done. I have seen a true veteran flyer wearing last
year's dirty, smelly, fermented laundry sitting quietly, alone, the entire flight. A real professional!

Make Out Technique

If you are with a significant other, start making
out, kissing and stuff as soon as you are seated.
This one is disgusting to most people. It takes a
bold, grumpy old man to break up true lust. This
is a top ten row-getter.

Van Winkle Technique

Find the first empty row and lie across all three
seats, resting your head on the aisle seat armrest.
Pile on the pillows and blankets. Spread your arms
and legs. You get great results if your mouth is open
and you are snoring loudly. Bonus, if drooling.

Drunken Sailor Technique

Loud, obnoxious behavior has its benefits. As
people walk through the aisle, make fun of them,
laugh at them, make wise cracks about their
mother, and generally be the type of person no
one wants to sit with. Be careful of old ladies with
large purses.

Irma says, "Don't even think about it."

The woman was all talent. Here she secures the entire row, executing the seldom-used "Cane Block Technique." Her strength and quickness amazed even the most expert boarding specialist.

Love Ya Technique
(Recommended for men only.) Get an aisle seat
and as passengers are walking past you, boldly
look them up and down, smile and occasionally
give them a wink. The women will think you are
hitting on them and most men don't really want
to know *what* you are thinking. When the pressure is on, reach over and pat the seat next to you
and wink. No one will take your invitation. This
one is a beauty!

First Time Technique
If you are sure the lady sitting in your aisle seat is
a rookie traveler, you can pull this easy one on
her. Show the large C on your ticket stub, point to
the C (aisle seat) on the overhead and tell her she
is sitting in your seat. At the first sign of confusion, tell her to quickly take the middle seat and
you will cover her mistake if the attendant comes
by. She might buy you a drink for helping her out.

Cripple Technique
As you enter the plane, begin to limp with your
"old football injury." Give the attendant a pained
look and ask for an aisle seat. When she asks why
you didn't pre-board, respond, "I guess I am just
too proud." Pre-board passengers that cheated to
get on first are suckers for knee problems and
usually will give up their seats. Guilt works!

Puppet Technique

Always carry a small, cheap hand puppet in your bag. Rock back and forth in your aisle seat, arguing loudly with the puppet. When you get to the point where you are losing the argument, bang the goofy thing on the seat in front of you.

 **Caution** Don't bang the puppet excessively; you'll hurt your hand, dummy!

This one is an automatic; usually good for the entire row.

Boxer Technique

This is a two-for-one skill. As you sit in your aisle seat, shadow box with the back of the seat in front of you. People will pass by, thinking you are nuts and, as a bonus, the seat in front of you will remain unoccupied. Throw in a couple of uppercuts, a few, "take that's," and you could get a whole section to yourself.

Star Date Technique

A little bonus technique that can be used in the event the guy sitting next to you can't seem to keep his mouth shut. Put your finger in your shirt pocket, opening it a bit. Lower your head to the pocket whispering, "Captain's Log, Star Date 007. Have secured passage on a crude, fossil fuel pro-pelled airship." When you see the eyes of the fast-talker bulge, make a few more entries into the Captain's Log. In five to seven minutes, your blabbermouth will seek passage via a back row seat. Be sure to note his defection in the Log!

Be "seat-smart" from the moment you walk on the plane. You want that aisle seat in the same row as the weirdo sitting by the window - because nobody wants to sit next to that strange dude. Always be thinking! Guard your comfort zone jealously. Wear your "nose and glasses," bang your head on the seat; always be convincing. A few minutes of idiotic behavior can result in hours of flying comfort.

Note Remember, it's not just about the seat; it's about the entire row—controlling the zone!

Idiot Management

You didn't perform the techniques you have stud-ied. What, no guts? You have failed your lessons! Not only is someone sitting next to you, but also they won't shut up. I know you are a timid rookie, so I'll bail you out with a few tips that can be used to get that motor mouth to move, or at least shut up.

Want some peace and quiet? Use one or two of these "mindbenders" on the clown sitting next to you and leave him speechless.

- *"Would you hold my bag? Be careful, it contains my poisonous snake specimens."*
- *"You know it's not my fault I pass gas; it's a stomach problem."*
- *"Sure feels good to be out of prison again."*
- *"Let's have a drink; the heck with my parole officer."*
- *"Sorry to be so rude; want a bite of fresh onion?"*
- *"Mind if I put my arm around your seat? Hand on your lap?"*
- *"So, how would you like a few religious publications from the Church of Satan?"*
- *"Like to see some naked pictures of my ex-father-in-law?"*
- *"Pardon my coughing; the doctors say people probably won't get infected."*
- *"Could you hold my carry-on for the rest of the trip?"*
- *"So, tell me about your sex life."*
- *"You know, I don't get the same urges since my sex change."*
- *"You know, I haven't worn women's underwear once since my operation."*

- *"Could you talk a little faster? I'm going to sleep when you are finished."*
- *"Wanna see my collection of toenail clippings?"*
- *"Hey, want to go to the restroom with me?"*
- *"Let me know when you go to the lavatory; I'll go with you."*
- *"What do you think of that flight attendants ears? Couldn't you go for a nibble?"*
- *"I don't know words so good. Could you read the sports section to me?"*
- *"No, I never use a handkerchief; that's what sleeves are for."*
- *"Bet ya I can name all fifty states. Tell me if I miss one."*
- *"Let's see who can drink the most beers before we get to Austin. You buy, right?"*
- *"How about a few games of scissors, paper, rock?"*
- *"Hey bud, would you scratch me right here?"*
- *"I think your planet is so beautiful during the tornado season."*
- *"I must enter a new human host body."*

A few of these treasures ought to quiet the jabber mouth next to you. At the very least you'll cause enough confusion such that he will be babbling quietly to himself.

Spirit of Irma

Listen up,

"You want my seat? Git in my row? Ya best be brave or stupid, cuz ya gotta get past my cane! Ya got an airline here that offers ya a fightin' chance to hold yer ground. Any American worth her weight guards her terrain. Trespass in my personal first-class section and you'll taste the genuine maple flavor of my fightin stick!"

Lots' a Luck,

Irma

"WE ARE ALWAYS LOOKING FOR PEOPLE WHO TAKE THEIR JOBS, BUT NOT NECESSARILY THEMSELVES, SERIOUSLY. SO IF YOU'RE A BIT OF A HAM AND UNUSUALLY ALLERGIC TO STUFFY UNIFORMS, VISIT SOUTHWEST.COM TO LEARN ABOUT JOB OPPORTUNITIES."

— SOUTHWEST AIRLINES AD
SOUTHWEST AIRLINES SPIRIT
DECEMBER, 2001

chapter 7

Spread Your Wings

Rules of Elbow Etiquette.

Considering the fact that the average knobby elbow is wider than the seat's armrest, it is apparent that sharing is not an option. Technically, the FAA Passenger Guide Manual, Section XXI, Part IV, Code 7a, "Rules of Elbow Etiquette" clearly states, "When seated, each passenger is legally entitled to half the width of their respective armrest(s)." Now that may sound official and fair, but half is as uncomfortable as none! And, if you are weird enough to complain about not getting your half, the attendant is sure to think you're just another whiner. You don't have to be uncomfortable, whiney or wimpy. It's your seat, armrest and comfort.

Regardless of where you are seated, an elbow battle is inevitable at some point in your flight. A window or aisle seat limits your adversaries to one. On the other hand, a middle seat creates a war zone on two fronts. Resting your arms comfortably is a luxury only the crafty, veteran boarding specialist is skilled enough to accomplish.

This section details the knowledge necessary to ensure a flight free of "slump shoulder." Either you take control of the armrest or you sit for hours, hunched forward, holding your peanuts. Be assured, this is not a kid's game or for the faint of heart.

The elbow battle is a full contact assault, utilizing one of nature's sharpest tools. Remember, folks, you have weapons and this is war. There is danger in the overuse of armrest control skills. Be aggressive, yet sensitive.

 **Caution** When you draw blood, you have gone too far! You play the game or you get hurt!

Controlling the Armrest

First, have a strategy. A middle seat doubles your troubles. You have learned how to get an aisle or window seat. If you failed to do so, you best loosen up your rotator cuffs before you sit down. When selecting an aisle or window seat, do so depending on your strongest arm. For example, right-handers should be sure the middle seat is on their right side. To hold your armrest position, always have your elbow resting at the upper end of the armrest. (You know, up by the ashtray that doesn't open.) It is easier to move down than up the armrest when jostling for position later in the flight. While waiting for the seat next to you to be filled, it is a tactical advantage to have your forearm covering the entire armrest.

The techniques that follow apply to any seat position, but are particularly important to those in the middle seat. The challenge is holding off two attackers at once. Sadly, there will be situations that may be insurmountable. If there are 350-pounders on each side, I have no help for you. If you're up against a pair of six-foot-sixers, you lose. If there is a pregnant woman involved, don't even try. Family members? Hey, you have to live with them; it's not my problem.

Gaining control is as much mental as it is physical. You know the feeling. That initial sensation of emotional rage you get when you suddenly notice the bum next to you stole your armrest.

Stay calm, hold your temper and concentrate on finding the right technique for the situation.

Armrest Control Techniques

Head and Butt Buck Technique
As you take your middle seat, move your head into the person by the window and your butt into the person in the aisle seat. When they indignantly move back, quickly plop into your seat and throw your elbows down on the armrest.

Note Be quick, as the openings won't last long.

Inch On Up Technique
If stuck in the bottom position, inch up slightly each time the person moves. Don't be greedy or too fast. A slow steady advancement should give you complete armrest control in twenty to thirty minutes. Studies have shown you have approximately sixty minutes before the average passenger realizes they have lost their position.

Your Drink Technique

Each time drinks and snacks come around, you've got a freebie coming. Be the first to reach for your stuff. When your sidekick reaches, quickly take the open armrest spot.

Note Be sure your tray is down so you can easily set your stuff down, ready to gain the advantage.

For You Technique

Offer the enemy your leftover peanuts or a magazine. Anything that gets them out of position will work. Keep the elbow on that side poised high and ready for action, again moving down as the opening occurs.

Recline Technique

Many times, reclining the seat creates an opportunity. Hit the recline button and then slide the elbows back with the seat. If you bump into another elbow, just grunt and take the entire armrest. Typically, people feel a recliner deserves temporary elbowroom consideration. That is a mistake you can never make!

Mad Man Slide Technique

If you need to fight off a real hog that takes up the entire armrest, you might gain control by using more of a wild, top down approach. Pull your tray down and flop your head on it, elbows at the very top of the armrest. Bang your head on the tray a couple of times, then slide back with elbows out, neatly gliding over the armrests. Don't worry, they will back off. As you sit back, in full control of the armrests, give a few hacking coughs, just to keep them off guard.

Are You Cold Technique

You are stuck in the lower position and can't seem to advance your position. Reach up and twist on the three air controls and push all the light buttons. It should only take a few minutes and your adversary will reach up to turn something off. That's when you've got the advantage!

Oops Technique

Make sure your tray is up. Drop your napkin, pencil, paper, or whatever in front of your target. If there is no offer to help, ask for assistance. Once they give up their spot, you win!

Irma makes her own rules

This technique was one of Irma's specialties. The "Head Whammy Technique" is extremely effective in securing an armrest. Irma recognized that most passengers fear an elbow to the head. They back off quickly. She was so quick and delicate with her elbows that she could split a lip and never bust a tooth.

Nightmare Technique

Lay back, pretending to be asleep. Have your arms
crossed in front of you. Make a low grunting noise
and jerk your elbows out and into the passenger(s)
arms. As you apologize for your "zombie attack"
dream, slip your elbows into position on the
armrest. Immediately go back to sleep; that backs
them off, in anticipation of another weird dream.

Look At That Technique

If you are having trouble with the window side
warrior, lean into her and point to an unusual-
looking cloud. As she turns in disgust, slide your
elbow into position. Then turn and work on the
aisle side guy with an onion-breath question.

Bugged Technique

Turn to the guy next to you and ask, "Excuse me,
could you lift your arm please?" Quickly take pos-
session of the armrest. Then explain, "I understand these things are bugged; I'll cover them so
you may speak freely." Lay back and pretend to
sleep, in case he tries to start a conversation.

Jelly Fingers Technique

As soon as you are seated, pull out your peanut
butter and jelly sandwich. Freely wave your gooey
and messy fingers as you speak to the lady next to
you. If she has the armrest, be sure to touch the

back of her hand with your jelly fingers when you tell her a weird joke. In no time, you will get the armrest. You can secure your position by leaving a bit of jelly on the top of the armrest.

Territorial Technique

As soon as you are seated, pull out your roll of orange tape and lay a strip across the armrest. Ask the guy next to you if he wants the top half or the bottom half. When he looks at you like you are crazy, take the top half and then rip off the tape. In the upper position, you are now poised to use some of the previous techniques to secure the entire armrest. Another advantage of this technique is that your weird actions may cause him to give you the entire armrest, in hopes you won't touch him.

Don't believe for one moment that only passengers play the elbow game. I have seen Southwest employees play that game with each other at quitting time, as they hit the door. Also, the gate people are experts, using quick elbow thrusts to control stray cattle trying to sneak on board before their turn.

In conclusion, it is your responsibility to control the armrest. There are no gimme's in this game. When it comes to your comfort, throw the airline "Rules of Elbow Etiquette" out the emergency exit. There can only be one winner, so use your weapons creatively.

Listen up,

"I've never met an American that didn't love the open spaces — with lots of elbowroom. I whip 'em fair and square and only resort to devious tactics when I don't get my share of breathin room. Ask any man who didn't offer me the arm space a lady such as myself deserves. This is the only airline in the industry that doesn't enforce the FAA rules for "Elbow Etiquette." These are my kind of people!"

Lots' a Luck,

Irma

"Just as we strive to offer you the Freedom to Fly, we offer our employees the Freedom to Have Fun."

—Colleen Barrett
President and Chief Operating Officer
Southwest Airlines Spirit
October 2002

Power of
the Peanut

Fly Southwest? Must be the nuts!

I'LL BET EVERY FLIGHT ATTENDANT has experienced the
wrath of a passenger who did not get his peanuts.
I've witnessed fellow travelers that missed out
on the snack toss and became downright hostile
because they didn't get their peanuts. We have all
heard the angry comment, "I paid for this ticket
and darn it, they're not screwing me out of
my peanuts!"

While snacking on my peanuts a short time
ago, I wondered if Southwest is actually pulling
another marketing ploy. Why is it so important

that they hook passengers on peanuts? Why is
Southwest known for serving peanuts? They may
pass out these terrific fishie, wheatie or pretzelie
things, but every snack combination has with it
peanuts. Before you get anything to drink, you've
got a bag of peanuts in your hand.

Southwest must be the industry volume leader
in peanut distribution (over 90 million bags
served last year). They served three times the
number of peanuts versus other snacks. Either
they own stock in Kings Delicious Nuts® or there
is another more diabolical reason.

In 1949 the National Institute of Nuts published a study that discovered peanuts have two
physiological effects on the human brain. First,
there seems to be a natural chemical in the nut
that induces a posthypnotic type effect. Upon
consumption, the consumer actually falls into a
mild suggestive state of mind.

 **Note** The more peanuts eaten by an
individual, the more vulnerable he is
to suggestion.

Think about it! You always get peanuts with
the snack, sometimes more than one pack of nuts,
and prior to getting drinks. The nuts have been
digested and the chemicals are in your system by

the time drinks are served. The drinks are "free," so everyone orders. The drinks are always served with a napkin. When you pick up the drink, your focus is on the napkin, you are under the posthypnotic effect of the peanut, and the napkin is saying to you, "Fly Southwest." Virtually everyone on the plane is ensnared in the old napkin-advertising scheme that slyly displays "Fly Southwest" in bold red letters.

Ask for more peanuts and the attendants run to serve you all the bags you want. A drink is never served without a napkin! This is weird! When the "Power of the Peanut" wears off, all the passenger remembers about the flight is "Fly Southwest."

Further research has uncovered the fact that alcohol increases the depth of the suggestive qualities of the peanut. Alcohol also increases the retention of the suggestive message. This explains why you get free drink coupons with flight tickets earned in the Rapid Rewards frequent flyer program. Once you fly Southwest, you will always feel the desire to come back for more. It's not the service, it's the peanuts! They have cleverly covered every angle in the exploitation of this uniquely special nut.

 **Note** Please note, Mr. Smarty Pants, feeding multiple bags of peanuts to the babe sitting next to you doesn't mean your suggestions will be internalized by an unwilling subject. Yet, combined with free drinks, either you could get lucky or you just might fall prey to the old reverse "Peanut Pick-up" technique—and she drinks free.

Nevertheless, amateurs should never exploit the power of the peanut. This is a highly specialized area of research, best left to the experts.

The second effect the peanut has on the brain is that of cognitive association. Once a passenger has fallen under the suggestion, he will always associate peanuts with "Fly Southwest." Eating peanuts at home, in the bar or wherever causes an unexplained mental flashback that induces an urge to buy a Southwest ticket.

If you have flown Southwest you probably recall this experience. Have you ever been at a bar, eating peanuts, when all of a sudden you blurt out to the girl you've been hitting on, "Come fly with me?" Snacking on peanuts at work, you look up at the boss and say, "Why don't you catch the next flight to Hong Kong?" You are watching the ball game, eating peanuts, and holler at your wife, "Fly into the kitchen and get me a beer." Deep in your psyche, the little gray cells are screaming, "Fly Southwest."

Irma was a real nut

With Irma's mind control expertise, the "Power of the Peanut" had no effect on her willpower. Here she displays her power to prevent persuasion by washing down several bags of peanuts with a half-pint of bourbon. Judging from the look in her eye, she undoubtedly dared the attendant guy to make an inappropriate suggestion.

There's more! When they open the door for deplaning, what fragrance wafts through the gate area as passengers exit past the waiting cattle? It's similar to the beckoning call of popcorn at the movie theatre. One hundred and twenty some people, having consumed over two hundred bags of peanuts, fill the air with eau de peanut scent. It's called "Peanuts Breath." The waiting passengers aggressively press forward as they subconsciously crave that first bag of peanuts.

People in the terminal get this urge to "Fly Southwest" as exiting passengers engage them in conversation. Should they converse with another Southwest veteran, the nostrils quickly identify the fragrance and an immediate bond ensues. Oddly, the message, "I LUV ya, man" filters through the brain as the unique aroma directs your lust to fly. This is powerful stuff!

Think of the aroma release in a peanut butter sandwich. Kids love 'em and kids fly Southwest. Every time they eat one, they start whining to mother about flying to granny's house. Once again, conditioning future behaviors. By the time they grow up, "Fly Southwest" will have been thoroughly etched in their brain. No wonder the airline is growing. I recommend buying stock.

What if they put free peanuts in a bag that says, "Fly Southwest" at the ticketing or check-in counters? Or strategically located fragrant peanut wagons throughout the terminal. Or coaxed the cafeterias into serving peanut butter sandwiches. Is there no end to the lengths to which this airline will go to gain passenger market share?

The peanut is so powerful that in September 1998 the U.S. Department of Transportation sent airlines a directive to create a "peanut-free zone" on their airplanes. It's true! It was the result of a Mayo Clinic study. My unreliable sources have informed me that Southwest was able to secure the only known copy of the study, thus protecting their secret from competing airlines.

The addictive power of the nuts has become so prevalent at Southwest that the company set up a special rehabilitation center for employees. Hundreds of innocent workers receive treatment for the misuse of the suggestive properties of the nut. It's sad, but there is always a price to pay for being number one.

Don't underestimate the "Power of the Peanut." When you open that packet of nuts realize you are entering the bizarre world of subconscious advertising.

Be especially careful of peanut exposure to your children. And, for heaven's sake, don't try this at home.

 **Caution** In any event, you now have the facts to make an informed decision.

This may appear to be an aggressive, sinister tactic by the Southwest marketing department, but they are to be complimented on their in-depth research into peanuts. They learned a long time ago that this nut holds the key to repeat business. Most other airlines have foolishly missed the mark by serving actual meals. Isn't that dumb? Do you think that deep in your subconscious you have ever yearned for an airline meal? It's the nuts, man!

Listen up,

"Why does any American worth her salt love peanuts? Cuz this country is full of nuts. That's what makes it America and ya gotta love it! Truth is, it only takes a handful of peanuts to absorb an ounce of alcohol. With all the peanuts this airline gives out, I can finish a half-pint of Wild Turkey® between Dallas and Houston and never get smashed. These nuts think of everything."

Lots' a Luck,

Irma

" SOUTHWEST SERVED 162.4 MILLION BAGS OF PEANUTS IN 2002."

—SOUTHWEST AIRLINES WEBSITE
FUN FACTS
DECEMBER 16, 2002 (UPDATED)

Get The Free Drinks
You Deserve

It's all about you, you, you!

You have worked hard, mastering the techniques to perfection. You deserve an ice cold, strong one. A *free one*! If you have drink coupons from the frequent flyer program, a free drink is simple. But that's too easy; no fun!

In this section, students will discover how to finagle drinks for free. No charge! Don't be shy. Remember, it's all about you, you, you. Have one on Herb.

Top Ten Free Drink Techniques

The key is sincerity. Friendly, caring body language gives the appearance of innocence. Women, this is where you shine. One free drink, coming up!

Have a Free One

You're sitting in an aisle seat, half-empty soda in hand. As the attendant walks by, sneak your recently "transplanted elbow" out far enough for her to bump it, spilling your "so-called whiskey." While you are screaming in pain and she is apologizing, demand an alcoholic refill. Good one.

Have a Free One

Push the call button above you and start coughing. When the flight guy shows up asking what you need, point to your throat, cough and mumble, "Peanut." He will ask if he can get you anything. Gag, cough, choke, and ask for a Bloody Mary. A real pro keeps coughing, usually good for two or three drinks.

Have a Free One

When they toss you the bag of fishies, scream and hold your eye. Complain loudly about the vicious, blinding orange fish throw. As the attendant apologizes, quietly whimper, "I could use a gin and tonic." Works best if you don't laugh.

Irma was a Wild Turkey

Unreliable sources indicate that Irma met Herb Kelleher in 1971 at the Southwest inaugural party in Dallas. Being the competitive lady she was and somewhat taken with Herb, Irma dared him to go with her on a "Turkey Hunt." Four hours and twelve bottles of Wild Turkey later, Herb, unceremoniously passed out on the baggage carousel. As Herb went around and around, Irma partied till dawn with the skycaps.

Have a Free One

Get the gal next to you or a spouse to order you a drink while you are "sleeping." When they bring you the "Seven and Seven," tell them you wanted a 7-Up. But, to be a nice guy, you will take the drink. A dejected look helps.

Have a Free One

Pretend you are sleeping and have your friend throw your Coke away. As it is being tossed, you wake up, screaming at your buddy that you had not finished your Rum and Coke. Usually the attendant will get you one just to prevent a scene. Along with a scream, give a very hurt "how could you" look. Women get away with murder using this one.

Have a Free One

On virtually every flight, the attendants need change for a five. Sometimes you get lucky and no one volunteers any change; push the call button. Tell her you will give her five singles for the five-dollar bill if you get a free drink. Works best on the second half of the flight. Easy one.

Have a Free One

If you are really desperate for a drink, go to the back of the plane and volunteer to pick up the garbage—for a free drink. It works once in awhile, but you still have to live with yourself.

Note Geez, have some pride!

Have a Free One

Flight attendants sometimes get confused as to which row gets what drinks. Keep your eye on the drink tray (you want the cup with the little red stick, dummy) and move quickly. If they hand you an orange juice, reach for the cocktail on the tray as you inform them that is what you "already" paid for. Then say sweetly, "You are working too hard."

Have a Free One

When you find your seat, dump all your junk on the seat and head to the back of the plane. Hang out until there are no attendants around. The lower left cabinet drawer as you face the restroom holds cold beer. It takes a veteran traveler 4-5 seconds to snatch six cans. Place them under your arms and slowly walk back to your seat like a robot.

Have a Free One

As soon as you are seated, ask for a glass of water to take your heart pill. Save the water. Later when you get the gin and tonic you ordered, drink it down quickly and refill with water. Inform the attendant you ordered a gin and tonic, not water. It's a two-for-one deal.

 **Caution** A little shady, but sometimes a guy gets desperate.

Have a Free One

This one is a freebie. As you know, every once in awhile you will experience a flight delay. While your first tendency is to get a tiny bit upset, instead, work it to your benefit. Keep your cool until you finally board the plane. As soon as you board, in your best whiny voice, cry loudly, "Gee, this flight is late; don't we get free drinks? Isn't that some kind of FAA rule?" Continue your whiny request for free drinks with every attendant you see. Try to get a few other thirsty passengers to whine in unison with you.

 **Note** This one works especially well because flight attendants will do anything to shut up a whiner.

Free One-Dining Tip
If you missed dinner and have already manipulated several free drinks, here's how to dine elegantly on all the peanuts and fishies you desire. Drunken passengers are a big pain in the butt for the attendants. After six or seven drinks, just tell them you may have had too much to drink. You need to have something to eat or you may throw up. You'll get all the snacks you want. May also get the guy next to you to move!

Yes, it's true; there's nothing like celebrating your accomplishments with a few drinks. The taste of alcohol is so much sweeter when you're drinking for free. Rarely will you ever buy if you work the techniques you have learned.

Here is a little story to end this section. It was a late Friday night flight to Las Vegas and the passengers were thirsty. The guy sitting next to me must have been saving his money for gambling because he was working the attendants all night for a free one. Finally, he waved the attendant over and said, "You know, I'm flying on my one hundredth frequent flyer free ticket; how about a free Scotch?"

Trying to be nice the attendant asked, "Really, when did you first start flying Southwest?"

Confident and cocky, he shot back, "It was August 14, 1970."

She smiled and walked away, returning shortly with a Scotch. As she handed him his drink she stated, "Sir, this is to thank you for being a loyal customer, and to help you to remember that Southwest first started to fly in 1971."

Sipping his cocktail, he turned to me and quietly whispered, "Works every time."

It's so humbling to watch the great ones work.

Spirit of Irma

Listen up,

"Real Americans enjoy a good belt of whiskey every now and then. By giving out them drink tickets; I'm thinking ya got an airline here that knows how to have a good time. As for me, there ain't been a day in my life I've been a quart low or a day when I ain't had a good time. Bring on them drink tickets, sonny! Ya know, these boys and girls seem dang serious about their jobs, but don't take themselves very doggone seriously. That makes 'em easy pickins. Now this is what I call one fun lovin' airline!"

Lots' a Luck,

Irma

"WE JUST SAY, 'BE FLEXIBLE AND IF YOU ARE LEANING TOWARDS THE CUSTOMER, RATHER THAN AWAY FROM THE CUSTOMER, WE WILL FORGIVE ANYTHING THAT YOU DO, '" SAYS KELLEHER.

—*SOLUTIONS MAGAZINE*
WINTER 2002
QUOTE BY HERB KELLEHER

chapter 10

Heading Out

Move it or lose it, buddy!

YOUR PLANE IS PULLING UP TO THE GATE. You've enjoyed a great flight—aisle seat, free drinks, peanuts—you had it all. One last piece of business remains; getting out of the plane as quickly as possible. You hustled to be first on, and darn it, you're gonna be first off.

Everyone is sitting impatiently, waiting for the little riot bell to ring. This is the time when flight attendants hide, for fear of being trampled. Slowly the plane approaches the gate. Passengers grip the armrests tightly, leaning forward, checking the competition. As the plane brakes to a halt, hands reach for belt buckles, briefcases in hand, bodies coiled and ready to spring for the overheads.

Even though there are a hundred passengers in front of you, it's important to be able to get just a bit closer to the exit door. You are rested up, you've made your plan while the plane was landing, and you are ready to jump into action. It just so happens there are a few techniques that will help you get one step closer to the door. Who knows, the extra minute you save could mean getting that open bar stool in the terminal lounge. It's worth the effort!

Heading Out Preparation Tips

The first consideration is to be prepared; poised for action. Others are fatigued; you are primed. As the plane slows prior to braking, have one hand on the belt release and the other hand on your purse or briefcase. Be sure to keep your elbows out wide so others seated next to you will give you plenty of room to work. If you are in the middle or window seat, lean toward the aisle to let others know you want out. Also, mumble such comments as "let's go," "come on," or "stop this big bird," thus indicating to others they best move it!

At this point, those around you know you mean business. Heading out can be quick and decisive if you follow the basic techniques.

Catch A Flight Technique
During the approach, notify a flight attendant that you need to catch a connecting flight to Bangladesh and you are running late. If there is a seat (a middle seat is okay) near the front, they will sometimes let you get your stuff and move on up.

Shifting Items Technique
Attendants always announce, "Be careful when opening overheads, items sometimes shift in flight." Tell everyone around you that it's important that you be the first to the overhead, just in case your snake collection accidentally opened.

Need A Hand Technique
If another passenger gets to your overhead first, proclaim loudly, "Lady, please let me give you a hand." People will let you move through the line to help. Take your item out first, step in front of the lady, then be nice and hand the bag back to her. You just moved up.

Line Lean Technique

When you finally get a position in the aisle, it can be tough to hold. It's like standing on a crowded ocean liner; people are pushing and waving all about. If they aren't sick you soon will be. As you stand your ground, lean into the guy behind you (or a cheater hitting you from the side) and thrust your carry-on ahead to hold the front space.

Note Veteran boarding specialists; don't be afraid to use the butt and push method in tight situations.

Straddle Lock Technique

As soon as the "riot bell" dings, shoot your leg forward from your aisle seat and step into the open aisle way. Standing with one foot in the aisle, thrust the other foot behind you such that you are in a straddle position facing your seat. In this position, you command a sizable area from which you can easily lunge toward your overhead.

Row Lock Technique

Another use for your bag or purse, once you have aisle control, is to toss it on the seat you just vacated. This effectively blocks others in the row from crowding you out of position.

Irma didn't care who she stepped on

Irma liked to use the celebrated "Metatarsal Crush Technique" to gain a clear pathway to the airport lounge. It's not a matter of size, but dexterity that counts.

Window Lock Technique

A window seat is a tough position to work from. You have to get movement from the middle seat passenger. If you are sitting next to a slow mover, politely let them know you've "gotta get going!" Get up and move your leg across in an attempt to step over them. Either they will push toward the aisle or you gain the advantage over one more person.

Switcheroo Technique

This one will give you some help if you are stuck in the window seat. As the plane is in descent for a landing, excuse yourself to use the restroom. As you leave your seat, just to be nice, suggest to the middle row passenger that they take your window seat. Hey, every step closer to the door helps!

Heading out is the last task the boarding specialist must learn to master. A quick and sure exit puts the final touch on a first-class flight. If you have taken your lessons to heart and worked hard at the techniques, you will soon have mastered personal customer service.

 **Caution** Others may consider you to be obnoxious, overbearing, rude and controlling, but you know in your heart those feelings are mere understatements of your true character.

Truly, like Southwest, you love the other passengers, but if they love you, they will get out of the way.

Strolling through the terminal, heading to Grandma's house or the lounge, hold your head high displaying the confidence only a professional boarding specialist can portray. This flight, and all future flights, will be about you!

Spirit of Irma

Listen up,

"When it's time to move out, an American gets off her butt and moves it! When it comes to gittin off the plane I see them flight attendants run and hide in the restrooms for fear of being trampled. Doggone if this airline ain't got the fastest in the business. I say good! Git 'em out of the way— I'm coming through. If I wanted to be patient and kind I'd a stayed in the Rest Home making them durn pot holders."

Lots' a Luck,

Irma

"WHEN THE PILOT HITS THE BRAKES ON THAT 737, I HIT THE OVERHEAD FOR MY LUGGAGE. A WISE PASSENGER WILL GET THE HELL OUT OF MY WAY OR BE TRAMPLED LIKE A DOG."

—IRMA
RETIRED CUSTOMER SERVICE CONSULTANT

chapter 11

The Best Travel Stories

You should have been there!

THANKS TO ME, YOU ARE FLYING IN STYLE, quite comfortable. You are in control, enjoying the warm glow of your newfound powers. Your moves are the envy of other passengers, who admire the smooth style of your techniques. Laughing, as passengers all around you perform for the enjoyment of the employees, you move effortlessly to the front of the line. You LUV to fly the fun-filled skies on Southwest.

Now that you are in a comfortable position to look down upon others, you will be entertained by a collection of the best Southwest Airlines stories ever witnessed by any passenger. Having flown hundreds of flights on this airline, I have witnessed the most bizarre events a relatively sane person could comprehend. These true stories just go to show—people are nuts!

Note Some of you may remember the old numbered boarding card system (1-30, 31-60, etc.). Many of these stories go back to the good old days, so they have been translated into the new A, B and C groupings currently in effect. I know; it's all so confusing!

Wacko Flight Stories

Flight: Phoenix to Ontario

The gate guy was trying to be funny on a Friday afternoon. As people pushed toward the gate he announced, "Today for fun, we will be boarding in reverse starting with the C group."

In broken English, this fat guy stretched over the rope, shaking his fist and yelling, "What doing, what doing? I wait hours to be here first. I kill you, I kill you."

Security delayed boarding for 30 minutes.

Flight: Chicago to Louisville

This crazy flight attendant was lying in the overhead (weird joke) and must have been quite startled when this grumpy old man threw his coat in the overhead and slammed the door.

Shortly, another attendant opened the overhead door. The trapped attendant popped his head out and asked the old grump, "Didn't you think it was funny that I was laying up there?"

The grump calmly replied, "Sure did. Thought it would be even funnier to see how long you had to bang on the door before someone let you out."

Flight: Seattle to Los Angeles

Everyone was jockeying for position at the gate. Irritated by the long line of aged, but not disabled pre-boards, a young lady at the end of the C group line walked away shouting, "This is crap!"

Apparently she must have hurt herself because the next time I saw, her she had an elastic wrap around her knee and was hobbling to the front of the pre-board line. Not only did she board early, but also received a hand from the gate gal as she limped on.

Flight: Cleveland to Nashville

All the pre-boards were on and the gate gal was about to do the A group, when this guy comes staggering through the pre-board area smelling like a brewery. He tells the gate gal he had too much to drink and needs to get on right away. He was immediately escorted onto the plane. The gate gal came back to a very angry crowd.

Sensing the hostility in the group, she got on the speaker and asked, "Are there anymore drunks in the group?"

All laughed and her life was spared.

Flight: Oklahoma City to Phoenix

I had to fly home with my six-month-old grand-daughter. As many women have experienced, I got no help or sympathy from anyone. Finally, I was able to pre-board by cutting in front of a wheel-chair, while the kid screamed endlessly. No flight attendants were interested in holding a pretty, but hostile, beast.

As I stood in the last row holding this scream-ing wildcat, I thought the flight attendant walking toward me was going to offer to hold her; instead, she merely stated, "Hold her up a little higher while she is crying; usually no one will sit next to you."

Had the whole row to myself.

Irma was a genuine lady

Irma not only expected good customer service from airline employees, she also expected good manners from everyone in the airport. Here Irma applies the "You Male Pig Technique" to correct a sloppy pick-up attempt. Any man not conducting himself as a gentleman would receive her undivided attention. Irma considered herself a lady, and expected to be treated like one. She also expected a man to buy a lady a drink at the bar!

Flight: Dallas to Austin

Just as the door was closing on the plane, a smarty-pants attendant, trying to be funny, announced, "Welcome to Delta flight 122 to Cleveland."

This old gal by my side jumped up and stepped over me as she reached for her stuff in the overhead screaming, "Oh no! I need to get to Austin. Oh, my gosh!"

She argued with the attendants up front as she tried to get out. Finally, the pilot came out and escorted her back to her seat, after he had assured her we really were bound for Austin. A new announcement was made.

Flight: Orlando to Houston

I saw the guy across from me drop a lime from his "pretty much empty drink" in the aisle next to him. When the attendant walked past, he reached for the lime, slightly bumped her and spilled a couple of ice cubes. She apologized and he got free drinks the rest of the flight. This guy was a pro!

Flight: Oakland to Las Vegas

This guy was either weird or drunk; probably both. As people boarded, he stood up in his aisle seat and invited people to sit by him.

He actually asked, "Would you please join me for today's flight?" People couldn't get past him fast enough.

I think the reason no one took him up on his offer was the way his toupee hung over his left ear. Intentional? Who knows?

Flight: Kansas City to Detroit

Well into the flight the captain of the plane walked down the aisle toward the back. This little old Kansas farmer put his hand up, and as the captain approached, he asked, "Are you the captain of this plane?"

Proudly the captain replied, "Yes sir, I am."

The farmer stood up, pointed his finger, and as seriously as a heartbeat shouted, "Well, who the hell is flying this thing?"

The captain smiled at him and respectfully replied, "Not me sir, my eight hours are up."

As the captain walked away the farmer mumbled loud enough for most of us to hear, "Wish I only had to work eight hours a day."

Flight: El Paso to Tucson

One trip through El Paso, I saw the Goat Herder Technique worked to perfection. These two old boys with cowboy hats and boots must have come directly from the Cow Pie Festival. They were talking loud and moved toward the gate with C group cards in hand. And, this is no fairytale; no one was within five feet. Sizing up the situation, the quick thinking gate guy took them with the pre-boards and sat them back by the restroom. The last two rows were sparsely populated.

Flight: New Orleans to Chicago

It was Friday night and the airport was full, the gate was packed and tempers were short. After the exit of the incoming passengers, the herd moved in for their convenient "OPEN" seating. The pre-boards were all on and the gate gal was about to announce the A group when this guy ran up to the front of the line, ducked under the rope and stood face-to-face with the gal.

Before she could say a word, he dropped to his knees and proclaimed loud enough for everyone to hear, "Will you please marry me? Or at least let me get on first?"

Thinking quickly, she turned to the waiting passengers and asked, "Well, what do you guys think?" The stunned group cheered and applauded—she let him on.

 **Note** This guy is my hero.

Flight: Jackson to Lubbock

I think it was a high school basketball team on their first airline trip. Expectedly, they were quite obnoxious. Finally, after enough passenger complaints this very small, cute flight attendant walked up to the biggest loud mouth and asked him to stand up. He seemed to enjoy being the center of attraction with this pretty little gal. He had the stunned look of a moron when she looked him up and down and shouted, "Give me 50 push-ups in the aisle, now!"

He did maybe 20, and then sat down, red-faced. The whole plane laughed at him. The rest of the flight was pleasantly quiet.

Flight: Chicago to Las Vegas

The flights to Las Vegas are the most fun on Friday nights. The Chicago group was well oiled by the Oklahoma City stop. A few of the loudest drunks in the back were making fun of all the cowboy hats boarding. Ignoring all the jeers, this big old Okie with a large Stetson quietly took his seat.

After about 30 minutes of harassment, this old boy slowly got up and walked toward the back. With his arms folded he flatly stated, "Problem with you northerners is ya'll got no teeth."

The biggest loud mouth from the windy city jumped up and shouted, "I got all my teeth, I ain't from Oklahoma!"

With a piercing glare, in an Oklahoma drawl he responded, "Son, you won't have any teeth when I get done with ya. And, you better be able to flap your lips fast enough to fly, cause I'm gonna throw your @*! off this plane." Another quiet flight.

Flight: Providence to Buffalo

The little boy was traveling alone, so the gate gal took him right on. Must have been his first flight. She got back to the gate and picked up the speaker-phone to announce that group A could board when a loud scream rumbled through the jet-way. The little boy burst through the door with a look of panic and turned to his waiting mother shouting, "They tie you down onto these big chairs, but I got away!"

I guess his mother got him straightened out because he didn't get away the second time.

Flight: Dallas to Seattle

The flight was in the air about an hour when a flight attendant got on the speaker and asked, "Would the person who had a cigarette in the restroom please come to the front?"

No one moved a muscle.

A few minutes passed, until a second announcement started with a giggle, "Would Cecelia Morowski please come forward to pick up your purse...and cigarettes?"

Yes, this one is true.

Flight: Portland to Spokane

The man had just sat down in one of the exit row seats when the flight attendant asked him if he was capable of pulling the exit door open in case of an emergency.

Proudly he looked up and replied, "Of course I can handle it, I was a paratrooper in the army."

The attendant smiled and said, "You just have to open the door, not jump."

He shot back, "If we crash do you think I will need to do either one?"

Flight: St. Louis to Louisville

In a middle seat, seated in front of me was this young lady fighting for space with two four-hundred pounders. One on each side, they had her surrounded. When it came time for drinks, the attendant asked her if she would like anything.

Disgusted, she replied, "Yes, I would like some air."

Flight: Boise to San Antonio

The elderly gentleman with a cane appeared disabled and weak, yet feisty, as he settled into his aisle seat in row one. To his surprise, a very large woman rudely stepped all over him to get the window seat.

In a fit of anger, he started hollering, and tapped her with his cane. She turned around, grabbed the cane and gave him a stern warning, "You stop that or I will keep this cane!"

His outrage abruptly ended when the flight attendant arrived and told him that if he didn't behave, he wouldn't get any peanuts. We all have a hot button!

Flight: Burbank to Salt Lake City

After a long wait, her patience ran out and she started banging on the bathroom door.

The door opened just a bit and the man inside snapped, "Just hold it a minute, I was here first!"

Not one bit embarrassed about his seated position, she pulled the door open and told him to hurry up. After a few minutes of verbal exchange, the flight attendant directed her to the back facility.

Oh yeah, this one is true too.

Flight: Los Angeles to Indianapolis

Here is a bold one. He must have been a traveling salesman from L.A. Things kept falling out of the overhead as he tried to stuff in his junk. Shortly, the gal in the aisle seat below had had enough. Giving him a dirty look, she slid to the open middle seat in disgust.

You guessed it; the salesman grabbed the aisle seat. She gave him a huffy, "Well, I never" as he stretched out to sleep.

This one is real. Later, though, he did buy her a couple of drinks.

Flight: Kansas City to Houston

The plane had made its way to the runway as the attendant stood up to give safety instructions. While she demonstrated the oxygen mask, the plane took a sharp turn, throwing her into an empty seat. About five or six seconds passed until she popped up with the oxygen mask on and frightened the little boy in the seat behind.

In spite of the peanuts, crackers, soda, airline pins and coloring books this kid cried and whined all the way to Houston. After landing, the kid ran up meet his mom and immediately told her how much fun it was to fly.

"They scare you, then give you all kinds of free stuff."

Flight: Phoenix to Reno

She looked like a small librarian, but she beat on the underside of the overhead compartment like a big-time wrestler. She kept banging at it until the flight attendant asked if she needed help.

Frustrated and a bit angry, she snapped "Why doesn't this open?"

Kindly as she could without laughing, the attendant said, "It is open, the door is up here."

I was there! I know it is true.

Flight: Tucson to El Paso

This old gal walked into the back galley. The next thing I saw she was spinning in a circle, pushing and pulling on knobs, pulls and latches.

Finally, she hit something and a drawer popped out, just about the time the attendant approached her and asked if she could be of assistance.

The elderly lady looked up and said, "Oh no, I'm just looking for the restroom."

Flight: Nashville to Louisville

About an hour into the flight, I observed water slowly dripping on the guy in front of me. A short time later, the attendant noticed the problem, moved the gentleman to the seat next to me, and proceeded to clean up the overhead.

While it was being mopped up, I asked the guy why he didn't hit the call button earlier, when he first noticed the dripping?

He smiled, "Too bad the attendant came when he did; that was some dang good moonshine."

Yup, it's true as well.

Flight: San Diego to Tucson

The herd was filing through the station in an orderly fashion as tickets and ID's were being checked. A young lady stepped up to the gate guy wearing a string around her neck. Clipped on the string was her license, ticket, ticket jacket, baggage claim and, hanging about six inches from the floor, her boarding card. The gate guy laughed and went right down the string to check out all the stuff. As he stooped down to the floor, she turned to the waiting herd with a self-righteous smirk, "With my new system, I have men at my feet all the time."

Flight: Louisville to Chicago

It was a particularly bumpy flight, and the landing was most entertaining. The grouchy old coot in front of me made sure everyone heard about the less-than-perfect touchdown.

Just before he exited the plane, he walked up to one of the cockpit people, exclaiming, "Now that we are stopped, did one of you guys check to see if the wheels were ever lowered?"

Apparently having taken enough crap, the captain snarled at the irritated old fellow, "We were pretty sure the wheels were down, otherwise it would have taken full power to taxi to the ramp."

Flight: Los Angeles to Kansas City

I was at the front of the line with my A card in hand when a gate change announcement was made, sending all of us to Gate 8. About fifteen minutes into the battle for new line position, another gate change announcement was made, sending us to Gate 17.

Eventually we boarded, everyone was seated and ready for takeoff. The door was ready to close when the attendant announced, "Due to the many gate changes, we want to make sure everyone on board is headed for Kansas City."

It must have been a pretty sharp group because nobody got up to leave. About two minutes later the cockpit door opened and out walked the pilot and copilot.

They gave the passengers a shrug, said, "Oops!" and walked out the door. I saw it happen – even I didn't believe it!

Flight: Oklahoma City to Phoenix

The dummy in front of me thanked the lady for the day's quick flight as he finished checking in. A bit surprised, she told him that Southwest flights usually are on time.

He smiled and said, "I was told it was a two hour flight to Phoenix, but the monitor shows an arrival time an hour earlier."

"Oh," she stated, "that's because of the time zone change. It's still a two hour flight."

He seemed a bit perplexed when he blurted, "Well, that seems to be false advertising."

"I'm sorry you misunderstood sir," she wearily responded, "but if you are looking for a one hour flight time, why don't you go to gate C1 and catch the flight to Amarillo?"

Either he thought it was an hour trip to Phoenix through Amarillo or he only had one hour to get anywhere, because the last I saw of him, he was in line at Gate C1.

Note Sometimes they let them all loose at once!

Flight: Salt Lake City to Boise

Upon landing, the flight attendant announced in a fit of humor, "Please check the overheads to be sure your belongings go home with you. Anything left will be sold at the Information Center by Gate B1."

Upon exiting the plane the little old lady in front of me asked the Attendant if there were good deals at the Center. The Attendant smiled and stated that she was just kidding about the sale.

"Oh," she mumbled, "I better tell my friends."

Sure enough, when I passed B1, there must have been a dozen little old ladies waiting for the big sale.

■ ■ ■

No doubt you are wondering if these stories are really true. I swear by the Oath of Herb that every story is true. After all, it's from these stories that many of the techniques in this manual were developed. You can see that Southwest employees are well trained to enjoy their jobs. Enjoy your new skills and have a little fun with those wild and crazy employees. Practice the techniques and master the game. As a boarding specialist, this is one game you are now prepared to win!

The end.

Herb, I was just kidding! I LUV ya, man, and Southwest is, indeed America's Airline!

Spirit of Irma

Listen up,

"Don't put me down and don't hold me back.
Americans are keen on bein individuals, be whatever they fancy. But these wacko passengers I
just read about in this here chapter were clumsy,
ignorant rookies. Fifty years ago if one of them
nuts was on a flight of mine, I'd a slapped 'em
upside the head a lick. Stupidity is un-American."

Lots' a Luck,

Irma

"TO PIQUE INTEREST, SOME FLIGHT ATTENDENTS ARE GETTING DOWNRIGHT
GOOFY. 'WE HAVE SOME FLIGHT ATTENDANTS WHO TRAVEL WITH UKULELES
AND SING THE FLIGHT SAFETY MESSAGE,' SAID LINDA RUTHERFORD,
SPEAKING FOR DALLAS-BASED SOUTHWEST AIRLINES."

—ASSOCIATED PRESS
THE ARIZONA REPUBLIC

Boarding Specialist Designation

Get some respect!

SWABS

YOU DESERVE SPECIAL RECOGNITION for the new boarding skills you have acquired. Get the respect a boarding professional of your caliber deserves. You can have airline employees begging for your autograph. All you have to do is pass the SWABS examination to prove your boarding knowledge and competency. This series of questions will challenge even the veteran flyer. Passing the exam is a sign of distinction that can be displayed with pride. Southwest Airline employees will honor your designation and step aside in admiration of your expertise.

OFFICIAL SWABS EXAMINATION

To gain your Southwest Airlines Boarding Specialist (SWABS) designation you must score one hundred percent on the test below.

 **Note** Do not sneak a look at the answer that is clearly posted at the end of the exam.

Directions: Circle the letter of the first answer (hint) that looks good for each question below.

1. Upon the successful completion of a technique you should never...
    a. All those below look good
    b. Apologize for the use of your skills
    c. Laugh hysterically
    d. Feel guilty for stylish execution

2. Flying for Peanuts refers to...
   a. None of those below make any sense
   b. Cheap Southwest tickets
   c. Psycho buzz after 10 bags
   d. Southwest cargo plane on a peanut run to Kings Delicious Nuts®

3. A true boarding expert is one who...
   a. Has the whole row of seats to herself, plus free drinks
   b. Gets on the plane last, then whines
   c. Apologizes for cutting in front of the preacher
   d. Is ashamed of her selfish behavior

4. All techniques have an excellent chance for success because people are...
   a. Sadly, all those below look pretty much true
   b. Usually wandering around the airport in a confused daze
   c. Unpredictable and tend to do weird things under pressure
   d. Generally nice, thus vulnerable to your highly polished skills

5. Your real goal is the "Comfort Zone" which
   is actually...
   a. The establishment of your own personal,
      well deserved "First Class" Section
   b. A myth in the eyes of untrained passengers
   c. A seat next to the restroom
   d. A bar stool and elbow room in the
      airport lounge

Scoring Your Exam: If you answered a. for
each of the questions you have earned the SWABS
designation.

Caution If you missed one or more
questions or cheated, you must
immediately retake the exam!

Successful completion of this exam entitles you to
bear the official **SWABS** certification card. Carry
the official card with the pride of a professional.
Don't be embarrassed to flash your card at
employees; after all, they don't even wear pants
(see ad at the end of this chapter).

Irma was certified all right, card or no card!

Irma didn't like the certification test, but she sure enjoyed testing the card. You can see here that the counter gal gladly extended Irma the privileges accorded such a designation. Of course, would you have had the guts to tell Irma she couldn't have whatever she wanted?

 **Note** Do not confuse your SWABS certification with the new Southwest business travel program called SWABIZ. The business thing is a marketing program designed to make business people happy, SWABS is a program of boarding techniques designed to make you comfortable!

"WORK AT A PLACE WHERE WEARING PANTS IS OPTIONAL. NOT TO MENTION HIGH-HEELED SHOES, TIES, AND PANTYHOSE. BECAUSE AT SOUTHWEST AIRLINES, WE DO THINGS A LITTLE DIFFERENTLY. AND IT'S OBVIOUS JUST BY LOOKING AT US. ESPECIALLY WHEN WE DON'T WEAR PANTS."

—SOUTHWEST AIRLINES AD
SOUTHWEST AIRLINES SPIRIT
DECEMBER 2001

Certification Instructions

Complete the final certification step by filling in your name and date on the card. Cut it out and display it proudly throughout the boarding process. Your boarding skills and extensive knowledge will impress passengers and have Southwest employees jumping at your every request. Don't ya Luv it?

CONGRATULATIONS!

Society For Airline Boarding Specialists hereby certifies that

_____

Name

having met with distinction the high standards of education and demonstrated knowledge established by this society has been certified as a SWABS:

SOUTHWEST AIRLINES BOARDING SPECIALIST

_____

Date

ATTEST: President, SWABS Association

Listen up,

"Americans hate tests! Whoever made up this stupid certification thing is a dim-wit. I certify people by not whacking them with my cane. No whack, you pass. If ya did something wrong, I'll cuff ya one, otherwise get back to work. This here airline runs a simple system that any dummy can understand. There's just too may rules nowadays. You want to certify something? Certify this!"

Lots' a Luck,

Irma

"FROM WHAT I CAN TELL THE DIFFERENCE IS IN THE LAUGHTER. IF YOU CREATE A PLACE KNOWN FOR LAUGHTER AND PLAYFULNESS, GUESS WHAT? CHEERFUL PEOPLE WANT TO WORK THERE."
EXCERPTED FROM *LAUGHTER OFTEN A SIGN OF BEST COMPANIES*

-DALE DAUTEN
KING FEATURES SYNDICATE
THE ARIZONA REPUBLIC

Think you are so smart?

Okay wise guy, you think you could write a better flight manual? Do you have weird Southwest stories, superior to mine? Have you developed techniques that could be considered improvements over those in this manual? A better sense of humor, perhaps? Think you are so smart?

Well, prove it!

I'll bet Southwest Airlines employees have some great Stories!

Let 'em rip!

Send your stories or techniques to one of the addresses below. No crap or stupid stuff; just a little positive reality! If I get enough decent ones, maybe I will revise this work of genius to include them. Remember, you are accountable for your own customer service. How do you take what you deserve?

send to:
Five Star Publications, Inc.
P.O. Box 6698
Chandler, Arizona 85246-6698

or email to:
flyingforpeanuts@FiveStarPublications.com

When you send it in, identify yourself so I can put your name on the weird stories. I'm not going to be accountable for your rubbish!

Other Fine Titles From
Five Star Publications, Incorporated

Most titles are available through
www.BarnesandNoble.com and www.amazon.com

Shakespeare: To Teach or Not to Teach

By Cass Foster and Lynn G. Johnson
The answer is a resounding "To Teach!" There's nothing dull about this guide for anyone teaching Shakespeare in the classroom, with activities such as crossword puzzles, a scavenger hunt, warm-up games, and costume and scenery suggestions. ISBN 1-877749-03-6

The Sixty-Minute Shakespeare Series

By Cass Foster
Not enough time to tackle the unabridged versions of the world's most widely read playwright? Pick up a copy of *Romeo and Juliet* (ISBN 1-877749-38-9), *A Midsummer Night's Dream* (ISBN 1-877749-37-0), *Hamlet* (ISBN 1-877749-40-0), *Macbeth* (ISBN 1-877749-41-9), *Much Ado About Nothing* (ISBN 1-877749-42-7), and *Twelfth Night* (ISBN 1-877749-39-7) and discover how much more accessible Shakespeare can be to you and your students.

Shakespeare for Children: The Story of Romeo and Juliet

By Cass Foster
Adults shouldn't keep a classic this good to themselves. This fully illustrated book makes the play easily understandable to young readers, yet it is faithful to the spirit of the original. A *Benjamin Franklin Children's Storybooks Award* nominee. ISBN 0-9619853-3-x

Letters of Love: Stories from the Heart

Edited by Salvatore Caputo
In this warm collection of love letters and stories, a group of everyday people share hopes, dreams, and experiences of love: love won, love lost, and love found again. Most of all, they share their belief that love is a blessing that makes life's challenges worthwhile. ISBN 1-877749-35-4

Linda F. Radke's Promote Like a Pro: Small Budget, Big Show

By Linda F. Radke
In this step-by-step guide, self-publishers can learn how to use the print and broadcast media, public relations, the Internet, public speaking, and other tools to market books—without breaking the bank! In *Linda F. Radke's Promote Like a Pro: Small Budget, Big Show*, a successful publisher and a group of insiders offer self-publishers valuable information about promoting books. ISBN 1-877749-36-2

The Economical Guide to Self-Publishing: How to Produce and Market Your Book on a Budget

By Linda F. Radke
This book is a must-have for anyone who is or wants to be a self-publisher. It is a valuable step-by-step guide for producing and promoting your book effectively, even on a limited budget. The book is filled with tips on avoiding common, costly mistakes and provides resources that can save you lots of money—not to mention headaches. A *Writer's Digest Book Club* selection. ISBN 1-877749-16-8

Other Fine Titles From
Five Star Publications, Incorporated

Most titles are available through
www.BarnesandNoble.com and www.amazon.com

That Hungarian's in My Kitchen
By Linda F. Radke
You won't want that Hungarian to leave your kitchen after you've tried some of the 125 Hungarian-American Kosher recipes that fill this delightful cookbook. Written for both the novice cook and the sophisticated chef, the cookbook comes complete with "Aunt Ethel's Helpful Hints."
ISBN 1-877749-28-1

Kosher Kettle: International Adventures in Jewish Cooking
By Sybil Ruth Kaplan, Foreword by Joan Nathan
With more than 350 recipes from 27 countries, this is one Kosher cookbook you don't want to be without. It includes everything from wheat halva from India to borrekas from Greece. Five Star Publications is donating a portion of all sales of *Kosher Kettle* to MAZON: A Jewish Response to Hunger. A *Jewish Book Club* selection. ISBN 1-877749-19-2

Passover Cookery
By Joan Kekst
Whether you're a novice or an experienced cook, Passover can result in hours spent hunting down recipes from friends and family or scrambling through piles of cookbooks. Now Passover cooking can become "a piece of cake" with the new book, *Passover Cookery: In the Kitchen with Joan Kekst*. You can create a new, distinc-

tive feast or reproduce the beautiful traditions from your grandmother's Seder with Kekst's easy to follow steps and innovative recipes from her extensive private collection. From daily fare to gourmet, "kosher for Passover" delights have never been easier or more delicious! ISBN 1-877749-44-3

Household Careers: Nannies, Butlers, Maids & More: The Complete Guide for Finding Household Employment
By Linda F. Radke
Numerous professional positions are available in the child-care and home-help fields. This award-winning book provides all the information you need to find and secure a household job. ISBN 1-877749-05-2

Nannies, Maids & More: The Complete Guide for Hiring Household Help
By Linda F. Radke
Anyone who has had to hire household help knows what a challenge it can be. This book provides a step-by-step guide to hiring—and keeping—household help, complete with sample ads, interview questions, and employment forms. ISBN 0-9619853-2-1

Other Fine Titles From
Five Star Publications, Incorporated

Most titles are available through
www.BarnesandNoble.com and www.amazon.com

Shoah: Journey From the Ashes
*By Cantor Leo Fettman and Paul
M. Howey*
Cantor Leo Fettman survived the horrors of Auschwitz while millions of others, including almost his entire family, did not. He worked in the crematorium, was a victim of Dr. Josef Mengele's experiments, and lived through an attempted hanging by the SS. His remarkable tale of survival and subsequent joy is an inspiration for all. *Shoah* includes a historical prologue that chronicles the 2,000 years of anti-Semitism that led to the Holocaust. Cantor Fettman's message is one of love and hope, yet it contains an important warning for new generations to remember so the evils of the past will not be repeated.
ISBN 0-9679721-0-8

Order additional copies as gifts for friends and family...

Name _____

Address _____

City _____ State _____ Zip _____

Phone (_____) _____

☐ Check enclosed   ☐ Money order enclosed

☐ Visa/MC/AmEx/Disc# _____ Exp.date _____

Name as it appears on card _____

Authorized signature _____

_____ Copies @ $9.95 ea. $ _____

Shipping/Handling ($4.00 for first
book, $.50 for each additional book) $ _____

Total enclosed $ _____

☐ Please send me a free catalog

Mail to: **Five Star Publications**
P.O. Box 6698, Chandler, AZ 85246.
www.FiveStarPublications.com tel **(480) 940-8182**
fax **(480) 940-8787**